BACKSTAGE AT BUNRAKU

BACKSTAGE

a behind-the-scenes

AT BUNRAKU

ook at Japan's traditional puppet theatre

by Barbara C. Adachi

photographs by Joel Sackett

New York • WEATHERHILL • *Tokyo*

Major portions of *Backstage at Bunraku* were published in slightly different form under the title *The Voices and Hands of Bunraku* by Kodansha International, Ltd. The text has been substantially revised, supplemented, and updated, and all photographs for the Weatherhill edition are new. Photographs appearing on pages 20–26, 49, 140, 143, 145 (upper photograph), and 146 are by the author; all others are by Joel Sackett. The title page design employs the crests of the Takemoto and Toyotake theatres. Drawings of the Bunraku stage are by Hidehiro Nemoto.

First edition, 1985

Published by John Weatherhill, Inc., of New York and Tokyo, with editorial offices at 7-6-13 Roppongi, Minato-ku, Tokyo 106, Japan. Protected by copyright under terms of the International Copyright Union; all rights reserved. Printed in Japan.

Library of Congress Cataloging in Publication Data: Adachi, Barbara C., 1924– / Backstage at Bunraku. / Based on: The voices and hands of Bunraku, c1978. / Includes index. / 1. Bunraku. I. Adachi, Barbara C., 1924–. Voices and hands of Bunraku. II. Title. / PN1978. J3A28   1985   791.5′3′0952   84–27016 / ISBN 0–8348–0199–X

Contents

Foreword

In most countries of the world the theaters of puppets or marionettes provide entertainment for children. Even the most ambitious companies rarely go beyond demonstrating how proficient they are at making little creatures of wood behave like human beings. Although sometimes they aim at satiric or even erotic effects that are intended to please adults rather than children, their dolls rarely enact dramas involving intense emotions or the expressions of sublime poetry. Histories of the theatre in Europe and America are generally written with hardly a mention of the art of puppetry.

The situation is quite different in Japan. During most of the eighteenth century, a time when the theatre was particularly flourishing, the leading dramatists wrote for puppets rather than for actors. Today, when these works are performed as Kabuki plays, the actors occasionally imitate the movements of puppets, thereby acknowledging their debt to an older tradition. The supremacy of puppets was such that one critic wrote, in about 1770, "Puppet plays are all the vogue, and Kabuki might just as well not exist." Not long afterwards, however, dissension among different groups of puppet operators and musicians, coming on top of fires and other disasters, so gravely weakened the puppet theatre that the dramatists shifted to Kabuki. This did not spell the doom of the puppet theatre, but it meant that the repertory, which formerly had been expanded every season with new works written by the leading dramatists, tended to stay the same, and performances consisted mainly of revivals of popular favorites.

The art of the puppet theatre came to be known as Bunraku, from the name of the man who took over the management of an important puppet theatre at a particularly dark moment in its history. He and his staff saved the theatre, but Bunraku was demoted to being a provincial entertainment, enjoyed by the people of Osaka but hardly performed elsewhere, even for the benefit of amateurs who enjoyed declaiming the texts of the plays. Bunraku could no longer compete for public favor with Kabuki.

It would have been easy for such a theatre to disappear. Indeed, in most countries of the world it probably would have disappeared when once it became financially unprofitable. But the Japanese have a special genius for preserving not only works of painting, sculpture, and architecture, but also intangible artistic traditions. Even the stately dances introduced from the Asian continent 1200 years ago are still regularly performed at the court and at certain shrines, no doubt because of religious associations they invoke. But Bunraku has always been a much more plebeian art, and without the support of the general public it cannot survive. Again and again in its long history it has been threatened—by dwindling audiences, by the deaths of senior performers, by the loss of its playwrights, or by the greater popularity of some new form of theatre. Bunraku has been saved in such instances by the remarkable devotion to their art shown by all concerned—not only the chanters, shamisen players, and puppet operators who appear before the public, but the invisible people behind the scenes who provided sound effects, costumes, wigs, props, and the other necessities of each performance. Barbara Adachi reports that the contemporary members of the troupe say of themselves, "We are Bunraku." And they are right. Not only are the people the indispensable elements of any performance, but they have preserved Bunraku even when the public seemed least appreciative.

When I first attended Bunraku performances in Osaka between 1953 and 1955, often there were only thirty or forty people in the audience, many of them looking as if they had once been geishas. The theatre was dingy and unheated even in winter. But the performances were extraordinary; the chanters, shamisen players and puppet operators who appeared at that time have become almost legendary figures. I recall especially my excitement on seeing *Sonezaki Shinju* (The Love Suicides at Sonezaki), a masterpiece by Chikamatsu, when it was revived in 1955 after about 250 years off the puppet stage. In the climactic scene of the play the unhappy young man Tokubei conceals himself under the veranda of a teahouse while his beloved, the courtesan Ohatsu, sits in the room above, talking to a prospective customer whom she detests. Despairing of finding any other solution to the misery of not being able to remain with the man she loves, she says as if to herself, "I wonder if Tokubei is willing to die." She thrusts her foot over the edge of the veranda. Tokubei takes it in his hands and passes it across his throat. It was a terrifying moment.

The same scene, when I saw it performed by Kabuki actors, left quite a different impression: Tokubei's gesture was less frightening than tender, even erotic. Both interpretations are valid, and they demonstrate the differences that exist when puppets and actors perform the same plays. The actor always retains something of his distinctive personality. We believe in Olivier as Hamlet or in Callas as Tosca, but with another part of our minds we do not forget completely who they really are. But the puppets, having no personality of their own, can become incarnations of the roles, of each line spoken for them. Unlike the puppets in use in other countries, the Bunraku puppets are often tragic in expression and bearing, and they have a pure intensity no actor could match. They borrow their motivating force from the three men who stand beside and beneath them, but they move of their own, as their tragedies dictate. To say they are incapable of motion themselves is true, but this is not the impression the perfectly coordinated movements of the three operators convey to us; the men seem like witnesses to the actions rather than the cause.

The spell of Bunraku is irresistible for anyone who allows himself to be moved. For some young Japanese, it is true, the stories seem remote, about people whose attitudes and morality are quite unlike their own. But this is true equally of the great classical theaters of Europe, and the magnitude of the success of their performances can be calculated in terms of the number and height of the hurdles which the spectators can be induced to surmount.

In 1955 many experts in Japan predicted that Bunraku's days were numbered. The death in 1962 of the master puppet operator Bungoro Yoshida at the age of ninety-three seemed to portend the end not only of an era but perhaps of Bunraku as a living art; it seemed likely to survive only by the generosity of local and national agencies that provided financial support. When I wrote about Bunraku in 1965 I expressed my fears that the art was in danger of suffering a general lowering of standards. I had heard people say that the younger generation of artists refused to put up with the rigorous training and even brutal treatment that their predecessors had assumed was necessary, and that new audiences, unacquainted with men like Bungoro, would accept a deterioration in performance without realizing what they were missing. Fortunately, such prophecies proved false: Bunraku is currently enjoying a prosperity that no one could have predicted even fifteen years ago.

Many books have been written by Japanese about Bunraku, and there are translations made by non-Japanese of major works in the repertory. Barbara Adachi, however, is the first to have written about Bunraku in terms of the people who make each performance possible. Each person involved, whether he captures the audience's attention by his powerful delivery of the text, or patiently repairs a puppet's broken arm in some obscure little room, does his work with the confidence born of tens of years of experience, and each is essential to the success of a performance.

In this remarkable book Mrs. Adachi has communicated the enthusiasm and knowledge that are the product of her years of watching Bunraku performances and her almost equally long years of personal associations with the men and women who make up the organization. No other foreigner, and probably no other Japanese, possesses the intimate knowledge of what goes on before and behind the scenery. She modestly disclaims any scholarly acquaintance with the texts of the plays performed, but having witnessed the chief works of the repertory many times she can tell, better than any theorist, what makes for excellence in a presentation. Of course, she describes what goes on in the presence of the audience, and writes with discernment about how chanters, shamisen accompanists, and puppet operators blend their talents to create a unified work of art, but her conversations over the years with the backstage people enable us to see how small factors—a special darning needle, a piece of an old baseball glove, or a yak's tail—contribute to the visual success of a play. This is the special distinction of a book (the original text now revised, updated, and expanded) written by someone who has gained the trust and friendship of a group of people who embody an art that is a glory not only of Japan but of the entire world.

DONALD KEENE

Preface

Over the last several years, I have had repeated requests for the book I wrote about Bunraku in 1977, which has been out of print for some time. An increasing number of people, both in Japan and abroad, have discovered the fascination of traditional Japanese puppet drama. This ground swell of interest in Bunraku provided the rationale for revising and updating my earlier volume, *The Voices and Hands of Bunraku*.

Also, there have been changes since I prepared the manuscript for the first edition. Although the traditions, basic structure, and character of the Osaka Bunraku Troupe remain the same, the group has a new home base: the National Bunraku Theatre of Osaka opened in April 1984. Since 1977, a goodly number of young performers have been added to the rolls, several members of the troupe about whom I wrote earlier have died, a few have withdrawn, two have retired, and the backstage cast has changed somewhat. I have a strong feeling of obligation to continue telling the story of the people of Bunraku today, and the changes and my growing appreciation of the troupe's artistry and dedication combined to supply me with renewed impetus to produce a new volume.

It was a fortuitous meeting with a talented photographer whose work I admired that made me decide that 1984 was the time to complete a new version of the book with new photographs. Joel Sackett's interest in traditional Japanese theatre has made the collaboration a happy and rewarding one and his photographs, taken in 1984, accurately convey the dynamic world of shadows of Bunraku backstage. Colorful though Bunraku plays usually are in performance, the true artistry of Bunraku performers and the atmosphere in which they work is, I believe, more accurately captured in black-and-white photographs than in color. Over the years, this opinion has often been reiterated to me by the performers themselves. Although superior monochrome pictures of Bunraku are scarce, they are apt to be truer to the performers' art: lacking the distraction of colors, black-and-white pictures can be richer in atmosphere, emotion, and, indeed, color. This accounts for my carefully considered decision to use monochrome in this volume. A small number of my own photographs, mostly of rehearsal and performance, are also included; the pages on which they appear are noted on the copyright notice page.

The people of Bunraku have been my friends for sixteen years and they have given me counsel, welcome, encouragement, information, and assistance of immeasurable value. Without their goodwill, there would be no book, but for any misinterpretations, I accept responsibility.

It is Faneuil Adams, the former president of Mobil Sekiyu K.K., whose enthusiasm gave me the initial impetus to write about Bunraku, and Mobil's financial support made publication of the earlier edition of the book in 1978 a reality.

I wrote the "Performance in Osaka" chapter in 1977 based on repeated viewings of many plays but specifically, the last scene of *Katsuragawa Renri no Shigarami,* the love story of Ohan and Choemon, as given in the Asahi-za. The new "Performance in Osaka" chapter included here, however, describes the opening scene from Chikamatsu Monzaemon's masterpiece, *Sonezaki Shinju,* a play that I have seen many, many times. The description is tied specifically to the performance in 1984 in the new Osaka theatre. The beauty of *Sonezaki Shinju* is striking and can be appreciated by neophyte and aficionado. The language, music, movement, costumes, sets and staging, as well as the story and its dramatic structure are such that both those who understand Japanese well and those who know not a word will find a Bunraku performance of *Sonezaki Shinju* an unforgettable aesthetic and dramatic experience.

The remaining chapters I have changed less, only adding information and clarification, particularly in the chapter entitled "Ohayo Gozaimasu." To all chapters I have, however, appended a section to bring certain descriptions up to date, thus enabling the reader to picture the people of Bunraku as they are today. Because accompanying the troupe when it toured in Shikoku for ten days in 1977 was a special experience, I have not changed my account of that unforgettable trip as distilled in "On Tour."

Although Japanese terms, in italics on first appearance, have been included in the text, English equivalents are usually employed, with the exception of *tayu* (narrator) and *kashira* (puppet head). Macrons are used only in the Glossary-Index. Names of plays are given in Japanese with an identifying title or gloss, not a literal translation, given in English at initial mention of the play and in the Glossary-Index. Performers of the Bunraku troupe are referred to by their first (professional or stage) names: this is general practice in Bunraku, just as *urakata,* the unseen people who work backstage, are referred to by their last names. Professional names for both groups are listed alphabetically in the two lists of performers, for 1978 and 1984, at the end of the book.

For many years of guidance and friendship, I thank the people of Bunraku. They have shared their traditions and their lives with me, their work and their fun, on stage, backstage, in their homes, and in mine.

It was the great puppeteer Monjuro whom I first met. Within a few minutes of our meeting in 1968, I was completely caught up by his enthusiasm, and it was Monjuro and his assistant, Tamamatsu (with the stage name Mon'ya at that time), who introduced me to their colleagues and to backstage Bunraku.

My introduction to Bunraku had come much earlier, during the first seven years I lived in Japan. I was taken to my first Bunraku performance in 1935 at the age of eleven. Bunraku performances were rare when I returned to Japan in 1946, but by the 1950s, Bungoro's performances in Tokyo were something to look forward to. By the 1960s, I was attending Bunraku regularly, and once the troupe started its appearances at the National Theatre in Tokyo, I seldom missed a program. Visits backstage became more frequent, as did trips to Osaka, other parts of Japan, and the United States to attend Bunraku performances. For the last fifteen years, regular attendance at stage rehearsals and performances in Tokyo as well as many in Osaka, both in the old Asahi-za and, since April of 1984, in the new National Bunraku Theatre of Osaka, have added considerably to my understanding.

In conversations in dressing rooms and workrooms, in explanations from the wings or during rehearsals, in reminiscences around the fireplace in the country or over a bowl of noodles on Dotombori, my Bunraku friends have been generous with their time and their knowledge. Every minute spent crouched backstage, kneeling in the *geza,* standing in the wings, chatting in the corridors, conversing on trains, planes, and ferries, and joking over drinks or coffee has been memorable. Listening to tales of past performers, participating in lecture-demonstrations on Bunraku in Japan and in the United States, and assisting in the troupe's preparations for presentations abroad have been stimulating experiences. Well over half of the members of the present Bunraku community have shared insights, experiences, and knowledge. I am grateful for the goodwill and trust the people of Bunraku have extended so openly to me. It is they who spurred me on to produce this new edition.

For assistance of various sorts, I also thank the staffs of the Bunraku Kyokai, the old Asahi Theatre, the National Theatre of Japan in Tokyo and the National Bunraku Theatre of Osaka. My special gratitude goes to Donald Keene; also, to Andrew Gerstle, Marty Gross, Hitoshi Hamatani, Tamotsu Harada, Sakinori Hirashima, Takabumi Hirashima, Yukio Hirata, Takami Ikoma, Stanleigh Jones, Atsumi Karashima, Sheelagh Lebovich, Kazuko Mori, Yasushi Oki, Andre Ranieri, Frederick Roach, Kim Scheufftan, Masao Shudo Setsuko Tanaka, Yoshiko Yano, Sotaro Yoshida, Toshio Yoshizawa, and to James Adachi, my beloved mentor.

The encouragement of my publishers, especially Jeffrey Hunter, Ruth Stevens, and Miriam Yamaguchi, has brought the project to fruition. I particularly appreciate the commitment of the entire staff at John Weatherhill, Inc. to the production of the new illustrations.

I hope this book will convey to the reader something of the warmth and light of the Bunraku world that my friends, the people of Bunraku, have been so generous in sharing with me.

BACKSTAGE AT BUNRAKU

The Tradition of Bunraku

Sometime just before 1600, a notable event occurred to change Japanese cultural development. Puppetry, narrative storytelling, and shamisen music were joined to create a new popular dramatic form known today as Bunraku.

The Japanese, like all people, love stories; storytellers had been plying their trade and developing their skills for untold generations, with the warfare of centuries providing them with rich material for epic tales. The history of puppets is more obscure, but in many parts of Japan the art of the doll manipulation was highly developed. It was in the late 1560s that a strange musical instrument resembling a mandolin, with a snakeskin-covered sound box, a long neck, and three strings, was introduced to Japan from the Ryukyus. Within a decade or so, this small Okinawan instrument was adapted to fit the skills and materials available to the Japanese craftsman and the needs of musicians, and the shamisen was created. An instrument of great volume and versatility evolved quickly. By 1600, the art of the puppet theatre of Japan had been born.

Dolls had been used in temple and shrine observances and street entertainments for many centuries. Recitation became an art as blind balladeers recited legends and historical narratives to the beat of a folded fan or the notes of the *biwa*, a Japanese lute. Buddhist chants, Noh recitation, and minstrels' tales of the Heike wars all contributed to the development of declamation as entertainment. With the recounting of the legendary romance between Yoshitsune, a hero of the Heike-Genji struggle, and the Princess Joruri, a mythical beauty, storytellers reached a pinnacle of artistry and popularity in the late fifteenth and sixteenth centuries. The princess' name was soon incorporated into the Japanese language to denote the type of entertainment provided by these storytellers. As techniques of musical and dramatic narration developed, the quiet notes of the biwa, beloved by the early spinners of tales, were replaced.

For accompaniment, the loud twangs, whines, and percussive sounds of the newly perfected shamisen were preferred.

Puppet drama—skillfully manipulated dolls in colorful costumes, narratives of dramatic and lyrical excitement, and the surprisingly articulate shamisen—developed at a rapid pace in the seventeenth century, at the start of the Edo period (1615–1868). Puppeteers, chanters, and musicians sought each other out. Troupes were formed to give plays for the townspeople of Kyoto, Edo, and Osaka and were summoned by emperors and shoguns for performances and honors.

This doll drama, or *ningyo joruri,* (literally, "doll, or puppet, storytelling") was a well-established theatrical art by the time the great chanter Takemoto Gidayu* founded his puppet theatre, the Takemoto-za, on Dotombori in Osaka in 1684. Gidayu's artistry made his name synonymous with the style of narration used for puppet plays, and the words gidayu and joruri are even today used interchangeably with the word Bunraku..

Gidayu was joined by another theatrical genius, playwright Chikamatsu Monzaemon, who had been writing Kabuki plays. After singular successes with Gidayu as narrator of his plays, notably the remarkably popular *Sonezaki Shinju* of 1703, Chikamatsu devoted himself to writing for the puppet theatre, turning out well over one hundred plays, many of which are today considered the masterpieces of the Bunraku and Kabuki repertories.

Chikamatsu's plays were often domestic dramas dealing with the tragedies and problems encountered in everyday life by the merchants and artisans of the time, particularly the townspeople of Osaka. This was a refreshing innovation, since up until then plays were removed from daily life, dealing with historical, religious, and legendary themes. Chikamatsu's tragedies were given stature by the beauty of his language and by the stylization that is both possible and necessary in a theatre of puppets. Chikamatsu also wrote historical plays filled with heroics and supernatural elements but distinguished from those of other authors by their realistic emotional scenes.

The combined genius of Gidayu, Chikamatsu, and the puppeteer Tatsumatsu

*The names of all premodern Japanese in this book are given, as in this case, in Japanese style (surname first); those of all modern (post–1868) Japanese are given in Western style (surname last).

Hachirobei brought ningyo joruri to its peak in the first part of the eighteenth century. The heated rivalry between Gidayu's theatre and the Toyotake-za, another puppet theatre built nearby in 1703, resulted in the rapid development of sophisticated puppet manipulation and in many innovations. Puppet operators who had hitherto been hidden while they held one-man puppets, about two feet tall, above their heads, created a sensation in 1703 at a performance of Chikamatsu's *Sonezaki Shinju* when they first appeared in full view of the audience, separated only by a translucent curtain. Even the curtain was dispensed with in 1705.

The chanter and musician first performed on a platform near stage center where they were hidden, with the puppeteers, behind an opaque curtain. Subsequently edged far stage left, they first appeared in full view of the audience on the right-hand side of the stage in 1705. The two were finally given their own auxiliary stage, the *yuka,* in this stage-left area in 1728, and the increased main-stage area was used for more elaborate sets.

By 1727, the eyes and mouths of the dolls could open and close, and hands could move. Fingers were further articulated in 1733. A year later, puppeteer Yoshida Bunzaburo devised the three-man system of manipulating puppets, which is still used for today's much larger dolls, and performers vied to outdo each other in skill and in dramatic effects.

Puppetry was a dynamic and important theatrical force for some seventy-five years, outshining Kabuki, but by the end of 1770s, with the death of some of the best narrators, playwrights, and puppeteers, Bunraku went into a decline.

On Awaji, an island off Shikoku, puppetry had remained popular local entertainment. A puppeteer from Awaji, Uemura Bunrakuken, came to Osaka to perform, and his troupe's popularity led him to establish a joruri school there in 1789. By 1805, he had organized a troupe of puppeteers who performed in shrine precincts. As interest in puppetry revived, a descendant of the puppeteer built a theatre in 1842 for his troupe's puppet plays.

In 1872, a puppet theatre was officially named the Bunraku-za for the first time. Since then the traditional Osaka type of puppetry has been called Bunraku and is considered synonymous with ningyo joruri. The term Bunraku is the word commonly used to this day.

The Meiji period (1868–1912) marked the second flowering of Bunraku, almost a century after the close of its initial golden age. Working as a strictly disciplined repertory company, puppeteers, narrators, and musicians of the time raised Bunraku to a high artistic level and were widely acclaimed.

Because of management problems, however, the Bunraku-za was taken over by the Shochiku Theatrical Company in 1909, and although a new theatre, also named the Bunraku-za, was built in Osaka in 1930, interest in Bunraku waned. The difficult war years, culminating in the destruction in 1945 of not only the theatre itself but also those puppet heads and costumes that had survived a fire in 1926, were followed by a brief spurt of interest. The Bunraku-za was rebuilt in 1946, but in 1949 the Bunraku troupe split into two groups, the Chinami-kai and the Mitsuwa-kai, over management policies. Before long, the two factions were performing together, however, and in 1955, Shochiku built a new Bunraku-za on Dotombori where joint performances started in 1956. By 1960, small audiences and the continued existence of the two factions of performers rather than a united group made the future of Bunraku appear bleak.

In 1963, a semigovernmental agency, the Bunraku Kyokai (Bunraku Association), was established to oversee the puppet troupe and the Bunraku theatre, the name of which was changed from the Bunraku-za to the Asahi-za. The two groups of performers were formally reunited under the auspices of the association and the Osaka Bunraku Troupe accepted the support of the Cultural Affairs Agency of the Ministry of Education, the city and prefectural governments of Osaka, and the Japan Broadcasting Corporation (NHK). The troupe performed more frequently and in more cities than ever before and, with growing interest and support, the new Bunraku Kyokai was soon well established. The inclusion of a special Bunraku stage in the structure built in 1966 to house the National Theatre of Japan in Tokyo gave added impetus. Today, the National Bunraku Theatre of Osaka and the Bunraku Kyokai jointly administer the affairs of the troupe and continue to receive the official support of the Ministry of Education, Osaka, and NHK. Although over one hundred amateur ningyo joruri groups perform in Japan today, only this Osaka company is known as The Bunraku Troupe, a full-time, professional, national repertory group of Bunraku performers.

The troupe's home base in Osaka was the Asahi-za until April 1984 when the National Bunraku Theatre of Japan opened there. The establishment of the new theatre caused a commotion in Osaka when it was first announced.

Changing the name of the Bunraku-za to the Asahi-za in 1963 had caused an uproar, and in 1984, Bunraku enthusiasts reiterated their disappointment over the loss of the traditional name for the puppet theatre. The announced move of the Bunraku troupe and its theatre from Dotombori to Sennichi-dori struck the feisty citizens of Osaka as even more outrageous. The puppets, the "ningyo" of ningyo joruri, had been part and parcel of Dotombori for centuries and the pride of Osaka. The solemn new name and the new location were criticized widely until the theatre proved accessible, comfortable, and successful.

The move to an elegant and spacious building was finally welcomed, perhaps at first with a sigh of resignation tinged with the frugality for which Osaka is famous, but ultimately with pride. The people of Osaka conceded that it was time the Bunraku troupe had a proper, permanent home and since the troupe had long been designated by the government as an "important national cultural asset," its base in Osaka should be worthy of its honorable status.

It was emphasized in the press that the National Bunraku Theatre of Japan stands only steps from the old Asahi-za. From Dotombori—the only "correct" way to approach a Bunraku play—one has only to walk along the quiet extension of Dotombori (some call it Higashi Dotombori), and take the third left to reach the new theatre. Not only is the present home of Bunraku minutes from the old Bunraku-za but the path from Dotombori corner is clearly marked: ornate brick-and-pebble squares set into the pavement guide one's footsteps from the Dotombori-corner bilingual sign, proclaiming "National Bunraku Theatre of Osaka" and "Kokuritsu Bunraku Gekijo," directly to the theatre on Sennichi-dori.

It was in Dotombori theaters that Chikamatsu, Gidayu, and Hachirobei perfected puppet drama, bringing it to maturity and early popularity. The modest puppet playhouse that Bunrakuken II opened shortly after the revival of the near-dying art of ningyo joruri, was located not in Dotombori, however, but in Kozubashi. The splendid National Bunraku Theatre of Osaka is only a stone's throw from the Kozu area.

The handsome, gray-tiled five-story building houses the main puppet theatre, a smaller hall, dressing rooms, workrooms and offices, lecture halls, restaurants, and a small Bunraku museum. The Bunraku troupe has settled into its new home and performances there have been greeted with enthusiasm and good houses, despite a lingering, disapproval of its surroundings of bars, lively hotels, and parking lots. As early as July 1984, however, Osaka cabbies were calling the grand new edifice the Bunraku-za.

Milestones in Bunraku history include the 1703 performances of Chikamatsu's *Sonezaki Shinju,* the realistic play that caused a furor in Osaka because it portrayed events that had only recently taken place there. *Sonezaki Shinju* brought acclaim to its author, ensured the financial success of the Takemoto-za, and led to Chikamatsu's decision to concentrate on plays for puppets. The play also served as the starting gun in the race for popularity between several rival puppet troupes. Chikamatsu wrote prodigiously, mostly the *sewamono,* or domestic tragedies, so loved by Osaka audiences even to this day. In November 1715, however, his great historical play, *Kokusen'ya Kassen* (The Battles of Coxinga) opened what turned out to be a record-breaking seventeen-month run.

In 1984, *Kokusen'ya* and *Sonezaki Shinju* were the plays chosen for the new theatre's July performances celebrating the glorious continuation of the ningyo joruri tradition in Osaka close to three hundred years after the plays' premieres. The performances of *Ashiya Doman Ouchi Kagami* (The White Fox of the Shinoda Woods) in August and September of 1984 specifically commemorated the two-hundred-and-fiftieth anniversary of the first appearance of three-man puppets: two puppets, each manipulated by three puppeteers, caused a sensation on Dotombori in virtuoso performances in *Ashiya Doman* in 1734.

The Bunraku troupe now appears in Osaka four times a year for fifteen- to twenty-day runs. It also performs regularly in four fifteen-day runs at the National Theatre in Tokyo, which was built in 1966 to include a hall specially designed to accommodate Bunraku performances. Annual performances in Kyoto and Yokohama are also regularly scheduled, and Bunraku is on the road from Hokkaido to Okinawa, in large cities and small towns, three to four times a year, for as many as sixty days a year in Japan. There are frequent Bunraku performances on television throughout Japan. The troupe has performed in the United States on several tours, and in Canada, England, Scotland, Austria, Belgium, Denmark, France, East and West Germany, Italy, the Netherlands, Sweden, Australia, and the People's Republic of China. More overseas tours are in the offing, some by small groups of performers within the troupe.

The Osaka Bunraku Troupe was designated an "important intangible cultural property" by the Japanese government in 1955, and over the years fourteen individual members of the troupe have been named "living national treasures" and honored for their skills.

The Osaka Bunraku Troupe today is made up of twenty-eight narrators who sing, chant, and declaim as they describe the scenes and accompany them; nineteen musicians who accompany them on the shamisen; and thirty-seven puppeteers. The men range in age from sixteen to eighty-five, and their experience extends from just a year to over seventy. A young narrator, musician, or puppeteer joins the troupe as the apprentice, or *deshi,* of an experienced performer. He may come with no previous training, or, as is more usual today, he may join the troupe after two years in the training course established in 1972 by the Bunraku Association at the National Theatre in Tokyo and now held at the National Bunraku Theatre in Osaka. Auditions of aspirants from all over the country are held annually and graduating classes have ranged from two to eleven students. All trainees receive brief preliminary training in narration, music, and puppet manipulation before specializing in a chosen field. Although each young man specifies his field of interest or experience upon entering the course, changes are not uncommon: one aspiring puppeteer was steered into a promising career in narration when his voice was discovered partway through his training, and another candidate gave up the shamisen when he showed marked aptitude as a puppeteer.

It takes three puppeteers to operate one puppet for all except minor roles. One serves as chief operator to manipulate the head and right arm of the puppet, one as left-arm operator, and one as leg operator. A puppeteer starts his training serving his master as an apprentice and general factotum, and learning to operate the legs. He then progresses to left-arm operator after three to ten years.

After one or two years' experience actively observing movement on stage, practicing intensively, and finally working as a leg manipulator with his master-teacher, an apprentice usually makes his stage debut operating a one-man puppet without legs (*tsume*) in a minor role, often in the company of other tsume. After several more years, his first performance as a head puppeteer using a three-man puppet will be in a small role, such as a child or a messenger, assisted by the customary left-arm operator and leg operator, both of whom are experienced puppeteers senior to him. Although the progression from leg operator to head operator is established by custom, the years spent at one level or another are determined by skill.

Puppeteers traditionally appeared on stage hooded and dressed completely in black, but as individual performers become known for their skill, audiences demanded that chief puppeteers appear with their faces exposed so that they could be recognized from the start. Since the beginning of the century, head operators have appeared barefaced and attired in elaborate stage garments for climactic and joyous scenes. Preliminary acts or important scenes depicting solemn or sordid events are still usually presented with all puppeteers hooded and dressed in black.

Ordinarily a single *tayu* (narrator) and a single musician perform for one scene or a portion thereof, appearing in formal attire on the auxiliary stage to the right of the main stage. In certain scenes, additional tayu and musicians perform on a platform extended onto the main stage, usually for dance scenes or the travels of lovers bent on committing suicide together. Occasionally, an extra musician will appear on the substage to perform on the koto or the *kokyu* (a small, bowed string instrument). Musical effects are created by offstage musicians hidden behind bamboo blinds in a small room above the stage-right entrance curtain.

No single man is designated the leader of the Bunraku troupe. Responsibility for the affairs of the troupe at present is shared by senior narrators Koshijidayu and Tsudayu and puppeteers Tamao and Kanjuro.

The unseen people (*urakata*; literally, "people of backstage") of Bunraku include the wig master, the repairer of heads, the costume director, and a variety of others who work behind the scenes. It is only through the joint efforts of every member of the Bunraku community that the tradition of puppet drama has been kept alive over the centuries.

Today Bunraku flourishes, with a vital resurgence of interest throughout Japan and abroad. Although the repertory consists almost entirely of eighteenth-century plays, sold-out performances are no longer unusual. Today's larger audiences are more diversified, drawing on every age group, class, and background and, because of Bunraku's exposure on television and on extensive tours, are no longer limited to city dwellers. Interest abroad in Japan's unique theatrical art grows apace and markedly increasing numbers of non-Japanese visitors attend performances in Japan. Puppeteers, dramatists, and dancers in many parts of the world today more and more frequently credit Bunraku with influencing their style of performance, and the works of Chikamatsu and other Japanese puppet playwrights have places in university drama courses abroad.

That Bunraku survives today, indeed that Japan is in the middle of what has already been called a "Bunraku boom," gives the lie to the voices of doom that recurrently described it as a passing theatrical novelty. Bunraku maintains its foothold as a literary and dramatic form, as spectacle, and as a demonstration of skill and artistry. The themes of sacrifice, loyalty, heroism, and passion in conflict with duty continue to move people's hearts despite the difficulties of a complicated, and often archaic, poetic language.

Bunraku might be described as the "art of threes": the spellbinding coordination of the three puppeteers manipulating one doll, the unity achieved by the three independent elements—puppet, narrator, and musician—and the intersecting lines of communication established between puppeteer and narrator, narrator and musician, musician and puppet, as well as between and among the trios of puppeteers. This interlocking and continual shifting of artistic triangles formed by words, music, and movement continues to fascinate, puzzle, and intrigue theatregoers.

The men who walk today in the footsteps of tradition and those who observe their path will see to it that Bunraku lives, just as it has for almost four centuries. In the words of one member of the troupe, "Every time one of us dies, there are people who say Bunraku is dead. We have never been more alive. We will continue to survive. We always have."

Performance in Osaka, 1984

There are two things that strike one about Osaka—the countless bridges and the Kansai dialect.

The speech of an Osakan cabbie sounds slurred and casual compared to the clipped accents of a native Tokyoite. Despite their friendly drawl, Osakans laughingly admit, they pepper their conversations with direct and positively un-Japanese references to profit and price, money and commerce. The last bastion in Japan of the abacus expert, Osaka now tingles with the beeps of the electronic calculator on which even noodle-shop delivery boys and school-girl shoppers tot up their bills: no longer does the city hum with the clicking of the beads of the wooden abacus that never lay far from the reach of any self-respecting Osakan of the past.

Who can count the bridges? Hundreds hyphenate the city, as any arriving visitor will notice from the air or riding on one of the many crowded express-ways. Winding through this commercial heart of Japan are the Yodo River, the Kizu, the Shirinashi, and the Aji, and crisscrossing these natural waterways are hundreds of canals, built for the most part three centuries ago during the golden age of Osaka's mercantilism. Along the rivers and canals came the logs, the rolls of silk, the reams of paper, the gold, the soy sauce, the coal, and, in particularly large quantities, the rice that kept the clerks of Osaka busy at their abacuses throughout the Edo period.

The city is still the trading hub of the nation. Cutting through the very center of the city is Mido Suji, Osaka's most elegant boulevard, which runs directly north and south. The branches of well-pruned gingko trees partially hide the banks, security firms, department stores, and shops that line the avenue's four kilometers. Through the gingkos' abundant summer greenery, their golden autumn dress, or their tangled cones of winter branches can be glimpsed the few remaining brick Victorian buildings of the Meiji period, the new glass and polished marble skyscrapers of today, and the classic facades of long-established retail shops.

Just south of Mido Suji's Dotombori Bridge, the pace and the mood of the crowds change. Steps are carefree and expressions turn bright as people cross Dotomboribashi, the demarcation between the world of business and one of the oldest amusement areas of Japan. Bordering the narrow canal that Yasui Doton started building in 1612 is Dotombori, the street that has immortalized his name. Along the six blocks running between Mido Suji and Sakai Suji and extending into the adjoining area, theatres, restaurants, bars, cafés, cabarets, music halls, and playhouses line alleys and arcades.

The word Dotombori has conjured up visions of pleasure in the Japanese mind for over three centuries, and as early as 1703, when Chikamatsu wrote the ever-popular *Sonezaki Shinju,* he included a line in which a clerk admonished his young soy-sauce shop assistant to stay away from the temptations of Dotombori. The line has elicited delighted and knowing smiles ever since. Dotombori, still a street of light and laughter, theatres and temptation, lives up to its reputation.

In the hour before noon the denizens of Dotombori shake off sleep and prepare for another day of showmanship. The shutters of the pinball parlors and the coffee houses grind their way open. The red crab over a restaurant stretches out its plastic claws their full four-meter length, motioning lazily to the yawning noodle-shop lad cycling along with the day's first orders. A janitor sweeps away the litter in front of the Shochiku-za, now a movie house but once one of the famous "five theatres of Dotombori." In front of the nearby Naka-za, three women with cotton towels tucked around their hair dampen the pavement with water tossed from tin dippers and point to the posters depicting the melodrama being performed there.

A giant blowfish, an unlighted lantern by day, swings softly in the breeze in front of a fish restaurant in the next block. At the corner of a tempura shop a bit further along the deserted street, the lifelike brown form of an enormous prawn, its body fully articulated, its tail realistically blue tipped, hangs four stories long and goes through its slow belly-dance. In the next block, a second-rate music festival and booths selling tawdry imitations of traditional toys and games are touted in the vacant lot where the Kado-za, another theatre, beloved for its vaudeville, once stood. In the last block of Dotombori, the amusement-park air seems to dissipate and the atmosphere becomes quiet. No hucksters cry out, no movable signboards beckon. An old pickle shop attracts leisurely customers. Shopkeepers' wives amble out into the street to squeeze the fragrant white peaches and tap the huge watermelons which lie in the fruit peddler's cart.

Near the end of the block a group of country sightseers stands gazing at the facade of what was yet another theatre. Above the entrance, white latticework hides the three-storied building, and a plethora of signs identifies the building variously as the former Asahi Theatre of Osaka, the Asahi-za of Dotombori, the theatre of the eighty-four-member Osaka Bunraku Troupe, the center of ningyo joruri, and, until the 1984 move into the National Bunraku Theatre building, Bunraku's modest national headquarters. One last sign directs the visitors to the handsome new premises only a five-minute walk away.

Built in 1956, the Asahi-za was the fifth structure to have been named the Bunraku-za, and the echoes of the hue and cry raised by the citizenry of Osaka when the building was renamed the Asahi-za in 1963 still reverberate. The older generation still speaks of it as the Bunraku-za, and aficionados talk of "attending the Bunraku Theatre on Dotombori" as if mentioning the new National Bunraku Theatre or the old Asahi-za by their proper names was an act of treason. But it was for twenty-one years at the Asahi-za and it is today at the National Bunraku Theatre that the people of Osaka have their Bunraku, the traditional puppetry for which the city is famous.

Today, beneath the old-style banners that flap in the wind on bamboo poles set directly in front of the theatre, three old men scan colorful posters and stylized paintings of kimono-clad figures in dramatic poses. A mother in blue jeans reads to her two children the calligraphy on the colorful banners. A young couple in matching designer shirts ponders over a seating diagram at the ticket window where a computer purrs, waiting to process a request.

Viewing the exhibits in the small Bunraku museum on the first floor of the theatre are people of all ages: matronly women in ample day dresses exclaim over displays of ornate costumes and stage props while young men with brief-cases peruse old programs. Fragile old women clutching fans and wrapped in somber summer kimonos like last year's cicadas waft slowly through the small room. A few men are dressed in dark suits and ties, but there are also uniformed students, girls with Snoopy satchels, young men with backpacks, teen-aged girls wearing floppy pantaloons and carrying elegant European-made purses, and middle-aged men in neatly pressed trousers and gray open-necked shirts. Several serious long-haired gentlemen in berets are studying texts, one of them nodding rhythmically as he mouths the words. A buzzer rings, and the groups push their way up the long flight of stairs, through the spacious lobby, and into the theatre.

The murmur of the settling audience is cut short. A sharp penetrating clack of wooden clappers sounds, then another and another; a faster sequence is accompanied by drumbeats and a few merry notes from a flute. A black-sleeved arm emerges from the right edge of the stage and embraces the striped curtain. To the sound of running feet, the disembodied arm sweeps the heavy drape open across the stage to the left where it disappears into the wings.

In the right-hand corner of the theatre, a wide single-paneled silver screen, set into the wall above the auxiliary stage which runs at a forty-five degree angle to the main stage, rotates to reveal a gold screen on its reverse side. On the dais in front of the screen, sitting behind a low lacquer lectern, is a man formally dressed in white kimono with a wide-shouldered, sleeveless dark blue vest. He is seated on a blue floor cushion at an angle to the audience, his feet tucked out of sight beneath him. Next to him, a man identically attired sits on a large purple cushion, a shamisen laid on the wooden floor in front of him.

The program contains a synopsis of the play, *Sonezaki Shinju.* It is the story of Ohatsu and Tokubei and was first performed in the Takemoto puppet theatre on Dotombori in the spring of 1703, less than a month after the actual events which inspired the play had scandalized the citizens of Osaka. Written by Chikamatsu Monzaemon, *Sonezaki Shinju* is in the domestic-tragedy genre and is the oldest of Chikamatsu's plays still regularly performed. It is also probably the brilliant playwright's most beautiful drama and one whose popularity has continued to increase since its revival in 1955.

The theme of lovers' suicide by a beautiful young courtesan and a shop apprentice affords many opportunities for interesting and graceful performances by both the male and female leads. The attractive sets—the environs of a temple at festival time, a teahouse in the licensed quarters, and scenes of Osaka and its bridges in the final journey—provide maximal aesthetic interest. Love scenes, a lively fight between a wily scoundrel and an attractive weakling, a sprinkling of comedy, well-sustained suspense, and the slow-moving, tragic ending give the play intelligible shape and variety. Beautiful and poetic language throughout, particularly in the final *michiyuki* ("journey") add to the play's appeal. *Sonezaki Shinju* is popular not only with Bunraku enthusiasts,who prefer it to the version adapted for the Kabuki stage, but also with neophytes who seldom attend traditional Japanese dramas, and with people who derive special enjoyment from listening to the moving and familiar lines and music. The plot, poetry, and music of *Sonezaki Shinju* have timeless, universal appeal.

The story is laid in Osaka and concerns the complications in the lives of Tokubei, a twenty-five-year-old clerk apprenticed to the owner of the Hiranoya soy-sauce shop, and Ohatsu, a charming low-ranking courtesan of nineteen who works at the Temmaya Teahouse. On the death of his father, Tokubei was adopted by his uncle, a soy-sauce merchant, who has now arranged to marry off Tokubei to his niece and to set the young man up in business. Tokubei's refusal to marry the girl infuriates his master, who had not only obtained the consent of Tokubei's widowed stepmother but had also delivered his niece's dowry money to the widow in her country home. The soy-sauce merchant, knowing that his nephew's infatuation with Ohatsu of Temmaya is at the root of the problem, demands that Tokubei repay the dowry money and then leave Osaka. Tokubei manages, with difficulty, to obtain the money from his stepmother but on his way back to Osaka with it, is persuaded by his friend Kuheiji to lend it to him for a few days.

The first scene takes place in front of a tea shop near Ikudama Shrine, where Tokubei and Ohatsu meet by chance and discuss their situation. Kuheiji appears and denies all knowledge of the loan from Tokubei. Angry to have been tricked out of the money by his friend in front of Ohatsu, Tokubei initiates a fight in which he is soundly beaten.

The second scene is laid in the Temmaya Teahouse where Ohatsu awaits a guest. In despair over the consequences of Tokubei's loan, and his uncle's disapproval and banishment of Tokubei from Osaka, melancholy Ohatsu grieves for her lover. She suddenly notices him hiding outside Temmaya's gate and joins him secretly. Called back inside, she proceeds to hide Tokubei from the proprietor, her fellow courtesans, and a guest, who turns out to be Kuheiji, in the famous veranda scene which Donald Keene describes in the Foreword. Kuheiji leaves the teahouse. After all retire, Ohatsu, having been vividly reassured by her lover that he will die with her in *shinju* (lovers' suicide), slips out of Temmaya with Tokubei.

The final scene is the poignantly beautiful lovers' journey to the woods near the Tenjin Shrine in Sonezaki, where Tokubei finally forces himself to stab his lover and then kill himself with the same dagger.

The theatre lights dim only slightly as the performance commences. On stage, the brightly lit set represents the gardens surrounding Ikudama Shrine. Stage right is a wisteria arbor laden with hanging clusters of lavender blossoms. Stage center is a tall stone lantern, in front of which stands a bench covered with a festive red cloth. A colorfully painted drop depicts a large lotus pond. A tea stall stands stage left, its paper shoji doors lettered to advertise its spring specialty, lotus roots with rice. From the shop's center entrance hangs a brown door-curtain; bamboo bars protect an open window further stage left.

At a forty-five degree angle to the footlights, the stage entrances at right and left are marked by black curtains decorated with identical interlocking white crest designs. The handsome Takemoto and Toyotake crests serve as an ever-present reminder of two men, as well as the theatres they founded bearing their names, who made important early contributions to the development of puppet drama. Next to the crested curtain on stage left, just at the edge of the set, a figure in black faces the audience. Visible only from the waist up, he knocks two wooden clappers together with a mighty whack and calls out, "*Tozai! Tozai!*" He singsongs a short announcement, giving the names of the play, scene, narrator, and musician, his voice slightly muffled by the black hood covering his face. The narrator seated behind the low reading stand bows over his script as the announcer calls; then his companion on the dais bows. The audience applauds. The hooded figure intones, "*To-o-o-zai, To-o-o-*" walking off the stage in midsyllable, the *-zai!* emanating from behind the crested curtain by which he exits.

Silence.

The narrator lifts his book to his forehead and bows again, then places it on the tasseled lectern in front of him and snaps open a page, patting it down firmly as he settles on his cushion. The musician next to him lifts up the shamisen, positions the soundbox on his knee, and picks up a large white plectrum.

Looking impassively over the heads of the audience, he strikes a series of fast notes, then pauses briefly. He launches into a bright melody in fast tempo.

The narrator's posture becomes more erect. He closes his eyes, readies his lips, and pronounces in rhythmic, moderate tempo the syllables "*Ta-chi-ma-yo-u . . .*" to the accompaniment of the melodic phrases of the shamisen player by his side and the gay festival sounds of flutes, gongs, and drums. His voice rises and falls, sometimes singing, sometimes speaking, occasionally chanting extended vowels, the pace of his delivery quick and his intonation melodic.

From stage right, a puppet, about half life-size, dressed as a man in a green-and-white checked kimono tied with a blue obi, makes his entrance. A sedge hat hides the puppet's face. Walking immediately behind him, a handsome man in a white kimono moves the doll in such a way that it appears to walk about the garden, then to glance at the open window of the tea stall. Another puppet, a boy carrying two black wooden kegs suspended from a wooden shoulder pole, follows the first puppet, his childish form attired in a dark kimono, his expression pleasant but foolish. He too is followed by a man in a white kimono who moves the puppet's arm to lower the kegs to the ground.

The first puppet gestures as he speaks to the child puppet who then repositions the pole on his shoulder. "And stay away from Dotombori," the man admonishes his assistant. The apprentice leaves, followed by the man in the white kimono and two other moving figures garbed in black.

All the while, the narrator sings to the accompaniment of the shamisen. This first entrance is the moment of surprise, almost shock. The doll is just that—a large, heavy doll. Its movements are stilted, artificial. The puppeteer is there also, in full view. Why? From this point, slowly, and before one is aware of it, a subtle transition occurs. The dolls—the puppets—come to life.

The puppet is moved to face the tea stall. In addition to the puppeteer clearly visible to the doll's left, there are two other human figures, totally covered in black, standing to the doll's right. As the puppet moves, the barefaced puppeteer also moves, but he remains expressionless and silent. The two puppeteers in black, their faces completely covered with chest-length, semitransparent black hoods, move in unison with him.

The audience's gaze is drawn in the direction of the open window where a pretty doll sits wearing a pink kimono patterned in red and green. The man in the sedge hat addresses her, "Hatsu, Hatsu!" he says expectantly. The

1. The Ikudama Shrine scene from *Sonezaki Shinju* in performance in the National Bunraku Theatre of Japan in Osaka. Tokubei is at left, protesting as Ohatsu is being led away by her patron.

2. At the end of a scene, a puppeteer prepares to sound the wooden clappers as puppeteer Tamao, assisted by Tamame and a leg manipulator, follow disheveled Tokubei offstage in a rehearsal of *Sonezaki Shinju*. The *tesuri* (partition) hides part of the puppeteers' bodies from the audience.

3. Ohatsu, operated by Minosuke, sits disconsolate as two other courtesans chat in the Temmaya Teahouse scene of *Sonezaki Shinju*.

4. Minosuke and Tamao check the positioning of their puppets in a final rehearsal of the important scene in which Tokubei signals his intention to die in a love suicide with Ohatsu. Ohatsu has a packet of paper tucked in her breast, and the puppet's mouth pin is visible.

5. Against a painted background of silhouetted pines, Tamao and Minosuke rehearse a love scene in *Sonezaki Shinju*.

6. Tokubei and Ohatsu proceed on their journey (*michiyuki*) to ▶ the accompaniment of some of Chikamatsu's loveliest poetry.

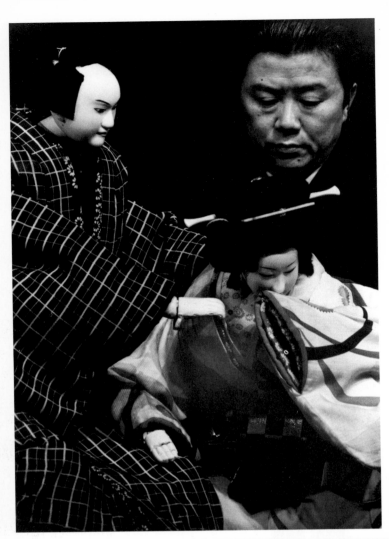

7 *and* 8. Ohatsu weeps and Tokubei comforts her after she cuts her hand in the tragic last moments of the play.

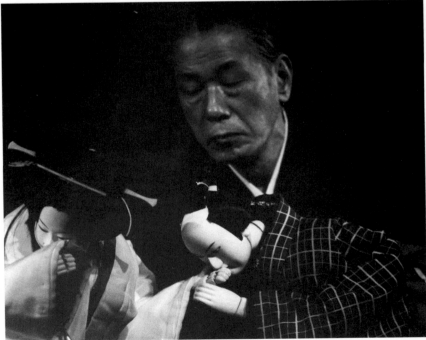

young woman replies in slow, soft tones, as she moves away from the window and into the garden, posing gracefully by the curtains at the tea-shop entrance.

"Toku, Toku," she says with delight as she approaches. Tokubei removes his hat and the two embrace. They move into sitting positions next to each other on the ground. Ohatsu speaks in a sweet sad voice to her lover and then shakes with grief and turns away from him. Near the edge of the woman's pink kimono sleeve, one suddenly is conscious of the movements of a bare human thumb. It extends from the thumbless black gauntlet worn by the black-garbed puppeteer controlling the puppet's delicate left hand with a black wooden armature that disappears up its left sleeve; gloved fingers move a string-operated lever on the rod as Ohatsu gestures. One's attention momentarily turns to how three human beings can manipulate one doll. Soon, however, one is conscious only of the overall flow of movements as the young woman doll turns back to her beloved and gracefully places one hand in his lap, then turns away to wipe away a tear, shuddering slightly as she cries.

The storyteller never pauses in his recitation, a long explanation spoken in quick staccato syllables in shrill, excited male tones.

On stage, Tokubei reaches over to comfort the young woman.

The shamisen notes are now in a pronounced minor key, and drum beats add emphasis. The lovers part, then draw close again. Tokubei interrupts his lengthy recital with tears, then continues. After a few more sentences, Tokubei weeps. Ohatsu puts a hand in his lap again, then the couple hold hands, she weeps, and he comforts her. Throughout, the shamisen plays along in strong rhythmic tones as the narrator's words pour out one after another with a definite beat. The masculine gestures of the excited young man and the graceful flutters of the woman's small hands create an ever-changing pattern of white accents, sometimes joined in twos or threes, sometimes separate or single.

"*Ureshi!* (I'm so happy!)" the young courtesan finally cries as she draws near her lover, relieved to hear that Tokubei has adamantly refused to acquiesce to his uncle in the plan for the arranged marriage.

Another amazement. The single narrator takes the individual roles of both characters as well as the narration of the story, his inflection and intonation constantly shifting. The shamisen adds counterpoint and comment to the narrator's voice and the action on stage. Narrator and shamisen are separate, yet one.

The puppets gradually assume life-size proportions. No longer do the faces seem small and immobile as they turn this way and that, glancing at each other, then away. The faces of the two principal puppeteers are ciphers: neutral, immobile elements present on stage only to be ignored. The four assistants are no more obtrusive than shadows. One postpones the question of how the illusions are created as one enjoys watching the lovers in animated conversation, noting only in passing that the unmasked puppeteer's hand is visible below Ohatsu's.

Ohatsu places her hands in her lap. A click of hand against hand, wood against wood, momentarily breaks the illusion, and one again is conscious of the larger-than-life puppeteer behind the puppet. The lovers move close together.

Suddenly, a flute, a drum, and bells sound. Then, with a metallic scrape, the stage-right entrance curtain snaps aside to allow a swarthy male puppet, dressed in a brown kimono and a short black-and-white checked jacket, to enter. Swaying and singing, the puppet staggers in. The doll is propelled by a frowning man in white kimono accompanied by two hooded figures in black who seem to glide into the room like shadows cast by the drunken doll. The slurred syllables of the song come to an end.

"Kuheiji!" cries Tokubei, recognizing his inebriated friend who is accompanied by two pals, the latter two puppets each moved in drunken gait by single, hooded puppeteers in black.

Kuheiji and Tokubei enter into heated conversation, Kuheiji speaking in rough, low tones which are followed by Tokubei's strident syllables. Tokubei shakes his friend on the shoulders and demands the money he lent him only to be shrugged off by the rough chap who shakes his head in denial of any such loan and pushes Tokubei off.

The narrator has added another voice to his repertory, and he becomes whiny, then gruff, accusatory, and derisive in turn.

Tokubei shoves the loan document at Kuheiji, then sighs in relief by Ohatsu's side, sure that the note bearing his friend's seal will end the misunderstanding. Kuheiji protests, laughs cruelly, then throws the paper to the ground. Ohatsu rushes to comfort Tokubei who breathes heavily in anger and frustration.

Forgetting the intricacies of the complicated situation that has excited the characters on stage, one intermittently returns to the matter at hand. How are the dolls moved? Clearly the unhooded puppeteer holds the courtesan doll from the back with his left hand, using his right hand to move hers, but the manipulations of the hooded man moving at the hem level of her kimono are still unclear. When the scoundrel turns to confront his friend, the three puppeteers seem to pivot around the doll as one and glide with it as a unit. There is a glimpse of two hands moving the puppet's feet. Tokubei resumes his prattle, whines, wails, and moans, stamps his feet, and finally attacks Kuheiji. Ohatsu rushes to intervene in the ensuing fight, but Kuheiji kicks her away and bystanders appear, two from stage right, one from stage left.

Suddenly the stage seems crowded. In addition to the three main characters in the play and five minor ones, there is an undercurrent of constant movement: three master puppeteers move in carefully controlled action while six shrouded operators in black add shifting silhouettes to the stage. In teams of three, the puppeteers create for each puppet not only a distinct personality but also a complex and visible nervous system. The supporting roles are filled by simpler puppets manipulated with minimal movements by single puppeteers barely visible in their all-black coverings.

The shamisen issues a series of staccato beats, one note, then a higher one, then higher still, as the fistfight continues. From the side, the narrator's voice shifts in range, volume, tone, inflection. To the signals, the punctuation, the underlining given by the shamisen player, the narrator speaks, whines, pacifies, insinuates, questions, cries, and laughs in dialogue and narrative. It is this combination of continuous movement and sound that draws one back into the drama, ready to ignore again the physical complexities involved in its creation.

A glance at the narrator reveals that he is using his whole body to produce cadences of rough laughter and then howls of pain. He leans back, then bends forward to slap the lectern; he turns his head from side to side, his voice rises and falls as the fight continues, his face turns red and glistens with perspiration. As Tokubei and Kuheiji trade blows, arms flailing and kimonos and obis flying open, the narrator becomes the aggressor, then the frail loser in turn. The slam of a wooden fist against a doll head reminds the audience that it is witness to a puppet drama but the human gestures of hurt and anger on the part of the victim recall the sting of the fist swung by someone thought to be a friend. The audience flinches and murmurs at the stage business, ignoring the six puppeteers, not puzzling over the mechanics but simply surrendering to the delight of observing human reactions portrayed on stage. The scene gathers momentum as puppets, narrator, and audience fill the hall with mumbled sympathy and embarrassed laughter at watching an unfair fight.

Suddenly from the teahouse window, a man calls out to Ohatsu to come away. He enters quickly and drags her away from the fracas, saying she might get hurt. Ohatsu scurries out, three puppeteers following behind the black-and-silver obi as if caught in Ohatsu's wake.

After a few more kicks and blows, Kuheiji leaves Tokubei sprawled on the ground and rushes off, stage right, followed by his two henchmen.

The musician plays a long sad motif punctuated with several sharp strokes of the plectrum which hit the strings and cat-hide soundbox in one guttural snap. Slower sad notes follow accompanied by whimpers and cries of defeat, fury, and frustration. Tokubei pulls himself up off the ground and approaches the three bystanders for sympathy but they shrug him off and leave. The sound of a distant solitary bell adds poignancy as Tokubei wipes his eyes, rearranges his disheveled locks, cleans off his kimono, readjusts his long obi, dusts off his hat and slams it back on his head.

In a final show of defiance, Tokubei rushes offstage to the accompaniment of the sharp cracks of the wooden clappers being struck together. A wave of sighs ripples through the audience. As the clappers sound faster and faster and the round platform carrying the narrator and musician rotates into the wall of the auxiliary stage, the striped curtain billows and sways its way across the stage, gripped at the edge by the hand of an unseen figure.

It is only when they leave the stage that the puppeteers come alive as individuals.

In the wings, stage left, chief puppeteer Minosuke hands a limp Ohatsu doll to its black-clad leg manipulator. The young man bows and utters a formal "Thank you very much" to his senior, then inserts his own arm into the left sleeve of Ohatsu's kimono and cradles the figure in his arms. Ohatsu's pretty face stares up at the ceiling. The young man is frowning in concentration beneath the front flap of his black hood, which is now tossed up onto his forehead; the copper wire of his face-protector catches the dim backstage light.

Minosuke's off-white linen kimono is damp with perspiration at the neckline. Another young man dressed in the standard black robe but unhooded comes forward and hands him a cold wet towel. Minosuke takes it wordlessly with a polite nod and wipes his glistening face that is pink from exertion. He steps off his wooden stage clogs that added eight inches to his height and slips into the elegant white-thonged sandals that another black-garbed chap has positioned next to the clogs. The figure in black who followed Minosuke offstage close by Ohatsu's left arm now accompanies him through the wings. The young puppeteer carrying Ohatsu trails behind but Minosuke pauses to reach back to brush a stray lock of hair from Ohatsu's eyes before heading for the corridor leading to the dressing rooms. He walks in soft, unhurried steps, cocking his head to listen to the action on stage.

A sharp metallic ring signals the closing of the stage-right curtain and puppeteer Tamao emerges in the wings, sweat dripping down onto the front of his crisp, pale gray kimono. He shoves Tokubei to his assistant, who barely has time to fold the front of his hood up over his head and grasp the doll. Tamao mops his brow with a cold towel handed him by a junior and steps casually down from his high clogs. "We have to move faster on that exit," he says softly without emotion. "Today was better but we have to convey Tokubei's anger, not only his humiliation." The young leg manipulator props lifeless Tokubei onto a bamboo pole next to the short backstage corridor leading to the stage-right entrance. Another assistant picks up Tamao's stage clogs and places them next to the puppet. The two young men chat softly as they struggle to tie on Tokubei's straw headgear at the proper angle for his next appearance on stage. Tamao walks with quick steps through the wings, discussing stage movements in low tones with the three young puppeteers who accompany him, gesturing and laughing silently. His expression remains pleasant, his eyes playful but his gaze turns from right to left, noticing everything—puppets, manipulators, sets—as he walks to his dressing room surrounded by his juniors.

Furious activity bursts out on stage. Young stagehands with long hammers tucked into leather tool belts buckled over the black robes that hide their jeans pull out flats, slide them onto the stage, hook them together, and then position pronged braces against the sets, hammering them securely against the wooden bones backing the canvas flats. The lone woman stagehand hammers a willow tree to the floor in front of a backdrop of a street scene. Two men, their black hoods thrown back, slide a lattice-work wooden gate stage front, then nail it into place.

Across the stage, narrator Tokutayu, in white kimono, blue winged vest, and slightly wrinkled matching *hakama* (pleated, divided skirt) shuffles slowly past the lineup of young narrators, dressed in blue-and-white cotton kimonos, who bow and murmur polite phrases to acknowledge their master's completed performance. Walking behind him, shamisen player Danroku speaks quietly with a junior musician already dressed in his formal stage costume for his appearance in the next scene. He turns sideways to avoid catching the stiff wings of his garment in the flat being shoved into place for the Temmaya Teahouse scene. A young shamisen player dressed in kimono runs by, carefully holding Danroku's shamisen by the base of its neck with a toweled right hand. His left hand grasps a small plush box, a large ivory plectrum, and a fist-sized bag. Puppeteers in black robes and several musicians and narrators in light cotton kimonos rise to bow and greet Danroku as he slides casually out to the hall backstage, his sandals only half on. Danroku stops once to greet Enza, an elderly musician who is making his stern, silent way to the revolving platform on which he will be swung out into the hall to perform.

The corridor from the wings leads past the prop mens' room with their orderly arrangement of some fifty items—smoking sets, cushions, swords, a dagger, a straight razor, a tobacco case, towels, writing brushes, a broom, several fans, an enormous lantern—laid out along five tiers of gray metal shelving.

Nambudayu, an elderly narrator, walks by, limping slightly and leaning on a sturdy wooden cane. He bows intently to the young men awaiting his arrival near the yuka but holds his head high and maintains a taut smile which softens his grizzled face.

Past Danroku's dressing room, from which come sounds of several musicians earnestly playing different melodies, are the rooms reserved for puppeteers. Here, master doll manipulator Tamagoro gets ready to go home. Seventy-four and almost blind, he continues to appear on stage, as he has for half a century, in such roles as the nagging old wife in *Keisei Hangonko* (Matahei The Stutterer), the play done in the matinee immediately preceding the evening performance of *Sonezaki Shinju*.

"Tamagoro operates from experience and by intuition," says Bungo, a puppeteer of forty-nine who was apprenticed to Tamagoro at the age of seventeen. "He wears the tallest stage clogs in the troupe, since he's about the size of most of the dolls he operates. Young Wakatama and I lead Tamagoro on stage to make his entrance. He picks up each stage clog and breathes on the top soles to dampen them just enough so that his feet won't slide around and then we help him onto them. He tucks his heavy glasses into his kimono and walks out on stage right on cue. To see him perform, you'd never know he was a man under five feet tall who cannot see."

Tamagoro's eleven-inch clogs stand near his dressing room. Inside, Wakatama folds up the old man's hakama. "Just the same size as the hakama worn by the puppets," says Tamagoro in his small voice. He walks out, using a cane and led by his wife.

Puppeteers

Bunraku puppets are about one-half to two-thirds life size (two and one-half to almost five feet tall) and weigh anywhere from ten to fifty pounds. They are operated by three puppeteers (*ningyo-zukai*) for all but minor roles.

The head puppeteer (*omo-zukai*) operates the head and the right arm of the doll. Inserting his left hand through the back of the doll's trunk, he grasps the headgrip (*dogushi*) to regulate the position of the head (*kashira*) and operates the toggles on the headgrip which control strings to raise the head, move the eyes, mouth, and eyebrows; many heads do not have mobile faces. While operating the headgrip with his left hand, the chief manipulator uses his own right hand to direct the doll's right arm. Hands and fingers on many dolls can also be moved by means of a toggle. The head puppeteer thrusts his own fingers through a leather strap attached across the palm of the doll's right hand to manipulate props.

The head puppeteer, who usually appears unhooded, wears a plain black kimono (white in June, July, and August) and a stiff, pleated skirtlike hakama over it. In special scenes, the head puppeteer wears the *kamishimo*, formal attire that consists of a stiff sleeveless vest (*kataginu*) of elaborate weave or design and a matching hakama worn over a plain kimono. He wears a white, thumbless glove on his right hand.

The head puppeteer sometimes appears, like his two assistants, hooded and dressed in a plain black cotton robe. He always wears high wooden stage clogs (*butai geta*) with straw soles, which enable him to work at a level four to twelve inches above his two assistants and to slide quietly across the stage.

The second manipulator (*hidari-zukai*) operates the puppet's left arm, moving it with his right hand by means of a wooden rod about fifteen inches long. This armature (*sashigane*) is attached to the doll's left arm with cords, which control a mechanism that moves or opens and closes the puppet's hand.

The left-arm manipulator wears the *kurogo*, a plain black ankle-length cotton robe with narrow sleeves, which is wrapped like a kimono and tied closed with a large bow over the right hip. His black hood (*zukin*) made of coarsely woven linen or cotton material, completely covers his head and neck, and his black gloves are

9. Minotaro and a left-arm manipulator concentrate in rehearsing a comic role, the intent gazes of both directed at the back of the puppet's head.

10. (*opposite*) The hooded puppeteers form a black backdrop for the puppet, with the main operator, on the left, directly behind the doll. (*above*) From a different angle, the leg manipulator can be seen standing behind the left-arm operator, whose fingers work the stringed toggle of the armature attached to a large male puppet's left arm.

12. A stagehand moves a sliding door to allow three puppeteers to enter with a large male puppet in *Sugawara Denju Tenarai Kagami*.

1. Minosuke and assistants just before stage shoji are
opened to reveal them performing a female role.

14. Tamao concentrates on descending to the lower stage level, known as the "bottom of the boat" (*funazoko*), in his high stage clogs during a summer performance of *Ashiya Doman Ouchi no Kagami.*

13. The doors are slid open again so that Sakujuro may leave the stage with two assistant puppeteers.

15. An ox-drawn cart on their left, ▶ a trio of puppeteers rehearse a scene from *Sugawara Denju.*

16. Rehearsing in the funazoko area of the stage, divided from the footlights by a low partition, are two three-man puppets, the puppeteers all unhooded, and two junior puppeteers with tsume wearing distinctively marked hats.

17. In the funazoko rehearsing *Sugawara Denju*, two puppeteers (foreground) listen to instructions from a senior, while Wakatama (rear, left) and Itcho run through a special pose—a princess escaping in disguise—without a leg operator.

19. Puppeteers in action with two puppets and props in a beach scene from *Kokusen'ya Kassen*. Only puppeteers whose last name is Kiritake **wear** flat-topped hoods; Yoshida and Toyamatsu puppeteers wear pointed hoods.

8. Itcho, on the puppeteer's high clogs, prepares or a stage entrance surrounded by stagehands.

20. A puppeteer and a stagehand watch action on stage, the first step
in mastering the complex blocking of a Bunraku performance.

21. In rehearsal, Monju concentrates as his puppet makes tea; Kame-matsu, assisted by his son, Itcho, in the easily recognizable Kiritake hood, manipulates an old-woman puppet resting in her sick room.

22. A child puppet is eased into position on the back of the male puppet operated by Tamao.

23. Tamagoro and his assistant puppeteers poised for a stage entrance.

thumbless. The left-arm manipulator wears plain straw sandals (zori) and is responsible for the props, which he hands to the head puppeteer as required.

The leg operator (*ashi-zukai*) is the junior of the three-man team operating the puppet. Dressed completely in black, hooded, gloved, and sandaled like the left-arm manipulator, the leg operator crouches to operate the legs of the puppet. It is he who stamps his feet for emphasis in violent and dramatic scenes. He grasps male dolls' legs by metal heel grips. Since female dolls do not have legs except in certain specific scenes (Ohatsu in the teahouse scene of *Sonezaki Shinju*, for instance), the leg operator pinches the inner part of the kimono with his fingers and manipulates the hem to create the illusion of movement. He bends his arm and clenches his fist to create a knee line.

The three puppeteers work together in total harmony of mind and body, although the three do not generally rehearse together at length for any particular role. The left-arm manipulator and leg operator are expected to operate in various combinations with any head puppeteer; the head puppeteer will similarly work as chief manipulator with several combinations of assistants during the performance of a single role, although only experienced junior puppeteers will be assigned to work with a high-ranking head puppeteer in a leading role.

Dolls are manipulated to reproduce commonplace human movements such as sitting, crying, heavy breathing, sewing, smoking, and dancing; these are known as *furi*. There are also *kata*, which are poses struck to display the grace of the doll and the beauty of the kimono line or to portray a dramatic climax of action or mood, such as victory, revenge, or determination. Kata are also used for certain stylized movements and consist of a succession of poses which combine to create certain types of walks or gestures ("strong-legged walk" or "raising arm as if throwing a stone," etc.).

Minor characters such as servants and soldiers are usually simple dolls called tsume operated without toggles by a single hooded operator.

In the small dressing room at the end of the corridor leading to the wings, Tamao, the chief puppeteer of the Bunraku troupe, starts to sew together part of the costume of one of the four puppets that crowd the room. Three young puppeteers whose lives as doll operators are directly under Tamao's supervision watch him carefully. At fifty-eight, Tamao is a slim, handsome man whose hair is only lightly touched with gray. A half-smile plays constantly on his lips. In a dark blue cotton kimono with a pattern of small white pine needles, Tamao kneels in front of the doll. The puppeteer's narrow obi is smartly knotted at the back of his trim, firm figure.

Tamao removes his glasses and leans back on his heels. "Mmm . . . that looks better. The obi was too high on his hips to look elegant," he mutters in a low, gruff voice, barely moving his lips. He removes the heavy white thread, needle attached, that dangles over his right ear and pokes it neatly into the sewing kit his junior holds out to him.

"The walk of blind Hyosuke in the last play is distinctive." His pleasant mumble is directed at the eager apprentice with rumpled hair who half-kneels beside him. "The point is to get across the idea of blindness when we make that quick exit through the rain. The man is in a rush, but his blindness adds an uncertainty to his gait. Today was better. Keep at it." The young man bows.

Tamao puffs thoughtfully on a cigarette. "In this world of Bunraku, every day is another day of training. From the day I started at fourteen until today, every day has been training, discipline, learning. And it will be study and practice, practice and study, until the day I die, even if I live to be a hundred. That's Bunraku—study, study, study.

"Those years as a leg operator are the most important. They are the basis for a puppeteer's entire career, the time to learn the fundamentals. Those were good years, those. The discipline was tougher then than it is now," he says with a pleasant grunt of a laugh, "but it's so much easier to learn when you're really young. The mind is impressionable, the body strong and supple. When Tamasuke, Eiza, and Tamaichi yelled at me, or even kicked me with their stage clogs, I never forgot what they were trying to teach me."

Tamao checks the toggles of the headgrip of a large male puppet head, making sure the eyebrows can be raised and lowered smoothly, the eyes closed, crossed, and turned sideways. He checks the main front toggle. "A bit worn but still good," he says, feeling the yellow silk string. He hands the head back absentmindedly to Tamaki, who, at thirty, has had two years of training in the program established by the National Theatre in Tokyo and almost four years with Tamao. Tamaki leaves with instructions to have the hair dressed by the wig master.

"It wasn't a matter of liking Bunraku or disliking it when I started. The man next door was a puppeteer, Tamasuke, and when I was fourteen he decided he needed an apprentice so he took me along to the theatre and put me to work. There I was, training as a puppeteer. I didn't know a thing about

Bunraku. I learned by listening, by watching. I wasn't taught. I just learned. None of this signing up because you've studied Bunraku and think it's wonderful. Just work. I don't know yet which is the better way to learn."

The sound of several people stamping in the hallway draws Tamao to his doorway. Puppeteer Minosuke is supervising a trio of young puppeteers as they practice in the narrow corridor. He taps the wrists of the leg operator who has a tense hold on the fabric-wrapped metal heel grips attached to the feet of the doll being operated. "That angle of your wrists must be sharper but not so tense—you can't maintain that tight hold properly. Loosen up."

Tamao nods, then leans out to give one of the young puppeteers a gentle shove on his right hip. "Keep those hips tipped forward, rear tucked under more, and bend those knees. The hips, the hips—it's the hips that matter. And you with the left arm over there. Move out of the head puppeteer's way when he steps back in that quick turn."

"*Chon . . . Chon . . . Chon, Chon,*" intone the puppeteers rhythmically as they move forward, then backward, in unison, all three pairs of eyes focused on the back of the doll's head. Minosuke kneels down to the level of the doll's feet to check their movements. Three more times, and then, without a word, the group breaks up. The limp doll is returned to a stand on the hallway shelf and the group of puppeteers disperses.

Tamao turns back into his room, slides across the tatami and picks up a pair of wooden puppet legs similar to those being used by the young trio. He checks the way the knee joints work.

"Those years I spent as a prop boy crawling on stage before I even touched a leg, that was when I learned the most. On stage in the black robe and hood but hidden from the audience by the stage partitions, I learned what props are needed and in what order. You know this character needs a fan here, a sword there, and you learn to hand them to the left-arm manipulator as he needs them. He's responsible for handing them to the head puppeteer, but it's you, down there on your knees, who's got to get them to the left-arm manipulator in proper sequence. You learn a lot that way.

"Opening and closing the curtains to the two stage entrances—that's another way to learn. Entrances, exits, different ways certain puppeteers come on stage, their concepts of a role. Old Eiza always did things the same way throughout the entire run of the play—I could count on it—but with Bungoro, you never knew. He made all sorts of little changes, depending on the mood he was in.

"When a young guy finally gets on stage, that's where he really learns. If he gets a minor part that doesn't have much movement, he can learn a lot just by watching through that black hood. Instead of thinking about what's for supper or where to stop for a drink after the performance, the important thing is to be aware of everything that's going on. One day, concentrate on how that older leg operator gets the legs moving like a tired old man. Another day, watch the chief puppeteer's stance. How does he tilt his hips to make the puppet seem young and lively, or strong and dignified? How close to the head operator is that left-arm manipulator? An operator watches and also absorbs these skills through his skin—the natural smoothness of the head puppeteer, the way the left-arm manipulator coordinates the left arm with the right arm operated by his senior, the spirited movements of an experienced leg man. The timing, how to work as one, you learn it in your bones; it can't be taught by words.

"Learning to use the fingers at the hem of the kimono of a female doll to create the illusion of walking or running is tricky. For the legless female puppets, if the leg operator moves the kimono hem too slowly, if the bump of the knee he creates with his fist is too low, the puppet isn't graceful, feminine, and alive. It just stays a limp doll.

"And then there's all that foot-stamping. The leg operator stamps his own feet, not the doll's, to create dramatic or realistic effects—the climax of a pose, a warrior striding out. Well, which foot first? Why? It's fascinating. There's so much to learn. Once the movements become automatic, you polish them to give them beauty and meaning.

"Those hours as a leg operator, from the first smack of the wooden clappers at noon until the last whack at about ten in the evening, they're great—every minute. Tough at the time, perhaps uncomfortable, but oh, the rewards!"

As he talks to his juniors, Tamao is persuasive, confiding, even cajoling. His usually slurred speech accelerates and tumbles out in animated Osaka dialect. He gestures often.

"Really, ten years is about right for the legs. I only got to do about four because I had seven years in the army and when I got back they set me to working the left arm pretty quickly. That was when I realized how much I'd gotten out of those tough years on the floor and the years with the legs.

"As a leg operator, the most important thing is to move with the head puppeteer, to place your hips correctly in line with his, although much of the time you must crouch and your hands are right up against his hips. Even in a crouching position, the leg man must keep his hips steady. No matter which part you operate, if you have your hips set properly, the doll moves correctly. Firm hips, firm doll. Wobbly hips, the doll flops around.

"When you move up to left-arm manipulator you have a chance to perfect your movements, acquire some skills of the head puppeteer, and in good roles, serve as the stand-in for the head puppeteer. I got some of my biggest opportunities that way. When the head puppeteer couldn't appear, I'd be told to go on for him. I was only twenty-nine when Tamasuke suddenly had to leave a major role because he'd twisted his ankle. He often did that on those high clogs. I got several other good roles when a head operator had to drop out, the sort of a role a man would not ordinarily get at twenty-nine, and a role I didn't get again for another twenty years. I'll never forget when they said I had to do a big role in a historical play. I didn't think I could, but Bungoro encouraged me and said of course I could. So I swallowed my fears and went out and did it. Good training."

Tamao's skills in operating both male and female Bunraku puppets had long been noted, but in March 1977 the government designated his talents an "important intangible cultural asset." A person who possesses such skills is popularly known as a "living national treasure"; Tamao is the second puppeteer to be so designated since the national program for recognizing artistry was initiated in 1955.

"I think there are more roles for male puppets that are difficult than for female puppets," Tamao says, "but I like both. For female roles there are basically only two categories of heads used: the young woman's head and the mature woman's head. But for male roles, why, just for old men there are six major categories, and each type of puppet head must be used in a slightly different way to get across the proper characterization.

"There's also the challenge of using one type of puppet head throughout an entire play for a man who starts out appearing cruel and unforgiving but ends up revealing he is really a stout-hearted samurai seeking the killer of his lord. I've got to move that Bunshichi head to show the man's good intentions, his conflicting loyalties, his hidden griefs. My movements of the head and right hand have to convey to the audience his unshed tears, his masked pain, or his disguised relief. Take the head inspection scene in *Sugawara Denju Tenarai Kagami* (Sugawara's Secrets of Calligraphy). In a few seconds, the puppet used for Matsuomaru must let disguised emotions show through; he displays recognition, grief masked by stern resolution, and the joy of loyalty maintained at great personal cost. The puppet head chosen suggests certain traits, but the puppet must be operated to show the character's motivation and feelings.

"The tayu's narration is essential, of course, but my movements must give his words that other dimension that makes them convincing. The tayu is an artist: he is interpreting, and I can't tell him how to express the feeling I too am trying to convey. The shamisen is the third force. Our work is distinct. Usually we complement each other well, but sometimes . . . if we're fortunate, we mesh perfectly.

"That's what we always aim for, that indescribable coming together of action, words, and music to create life. That's the real meaning of Bunraku, the whole point. If we aren't together, the beauty of the play and the meaning of our skills are lost. The puppet's movements become simply those of a doll prancing to music. Puppeteer, tayu, and shamisen player join together to create a dramatic and aesthetic experience and to peer into the depths of human emotions with the audience."

Tamao works to adjust the kimono folds of the tattered costume used for Shunkan, the priest in exile who gives up his chance to return from banishment in *Heike Nyogo no Shima* (The Heike Island of Exile) by Chikamatsu. "A big puppet in heavy armor is much easier to operate than a light doll like this. A noble in court dress about to commit *seppuku* (suicide by ritual disembowelment) like Hangan in *Kanadehon Chushingura* (The Forty-Seven Ronin) is harder to do than a warrior telling of a victory in battle, because the former must express grief.

"What is at the bottom of an exile's heart? What are Hangan's emotions as he faces suicide? The artistry of portraying the depth of a man's soul, that's the biggest challenge a puppeteer has.

"A puppeteer doesn't imitate life, but the way the puppet moves must reflect life, not merely be lifelike. The puppet has no words, but shoulders can be moved in bravado or resignation, arms raised in horror or threat, hands clenched in determination or opened in insult. A puppet's gait can express weariness or joyous expectation, the innocence of youth or the despair of old age. It is the artistry of revealing the *hara*—the inner center of emotion and spirit—that the chief puppeteer wants to attain as he works with the left-arm operator and the leg operator.

"For female roles," Tamao continues, "one of the most difficult parts is when a woman stands at length and speaks with great emotion. The female puppet has no legs but must be held in standing position and moved enough so that the doll has substance and is believable as a woman of elegance and dignity. For female roles, strength and grandeur are harder to achieve than youthful grace; sadness and loneliness are more difficult than joy and passion. It's a lot easier operating one of those female dolls seated, and gossiping or flirting. It takes all the strength I can summon to hold up a light female puppet in such a way that she seems to stand firmly on the ground, her deep-seated sorrow credible.

"One of the most important traits a puppeteer wants to get across in a female puppet is her charm. In the case of a young woman, whether a young girl, a youngish wife, or a prostitute, there is a sensuous quality to be conveyed. For an older woman, this quality must be less physical; it must be a mature and natural charm that shines through and gives her a special aura of elegance and mature beauty.

"The charms of a courtesan and that of her rival, a sweet young wife who has been deserted, are quite different, but there is a certain sexuality in both that the puppeteer must portray. It is not enough for me to dip the doll's shoulder or to place her right hand provocatively in her lap. Those charming gestures will simply not work for every role. They must be worked out according to character, age, social position. There are certain conventions of gesture and pose, but there is much beyond that that must be varied.

"The charm exuded by a handsome young man is still another thing. I particularly like the roll of Tokubei, the determined lover in Chikamatsu's *Sonezaki Shinju*. He is so attractive to Ohatsu, a low-ranking prostitute of the licensed quarters, that she is willing to die with him, but his love-crazed charm and determination have hints of weakness and are quite different from that of a handsome young man who commits suicide for the cause of his lord. The same puppet head is used in both roles, but the way the puppet is manipulated determines the different personalities. Tokubei is set on marrying the woman he loves but he wails and moans about his fate the way no samurai would. He has the determination to die in the end, however, so he cannot be considered a complete weakling.

"Being a Bunraku puppeteer involves more than just learning to move the legs, jiggle the toggles, tilt the headgrip, grip a sword, fling out an arm. The role has to be studied. What is behind the words? I build up a role slowly and prefer a restrained style without excess movement. The portrayal must come from the depths of my being, my hara. I use my hips and my arms to confer strength on the puppet, to pour strength into the doll. It must move, to show emotion and motivation, not just flail around on the stage.

"As I grow older, I play many roles I did a decade ago but in a different way. My understanding of the role has grown and will continue to. Study, study, all my life. What I did as a young man because of physical strength and enthusiasm I hope to develop into artistry and finesse as an old man. This is the excitement and the joy of being a puppeteer."

Tamao flexes his fingers. The middle finger of his left hand is noticeably thicker than the others. He rubs a callus on his left palm.

"Bunraku is deep, very deep. There is much below the surface of any play that must be studied. People say it's so wonderful that I've become a 'living national treasure.' Well, I'm very honored that I've finally reached the moon, so to speak. But there's a whole big universe out there to explore. I want to go on to Mars, I want to go to all those other planets spinning around out there in the universe, to study each one. There's so much to explore, that whole big world of Bunraku. I'm not there yet. No, not yet. There's so much to learn."

In 1984, Tamao at sixty-five is handsomer than ever, his hair now quite gray. His joy in his work is clearly evident during rehearsals. Additionally, he exudes a happy pride in the progress made by several of his apprentices in their thirties. His grandson's decision to become a puppeteer seems to have endowed Tamao with renewed energy and dedication.

He continues to take his role as senior director and advisor seriously, whether he is adjusting a leg manipulator's arm, a left-arm operator's hips, a carpenter's saw, or a set painter's brush. His sincerity and warmth pervade the atmosphere backstage and his professionalism and skill make him one of Bunraku's best and most popular performers. It is his optimistic cooperation with his colleagues and his whole-hearted commitment to every detail of each Bunraku performance that give an almost palpable stability to the troupe's activities.

Narrators

To the left of the main stage is the auxiliary stage, or *yuka,* with a revolving circular dais on which the narrators (tayu) and shamisen players perform throughout the play. The tayu sets the scene, describes the emotions of the characters, recites the narrative, and delivers all the dialogue. Only in special scenes are there several tayu, each one taking a role, or all singing in chorus. The tayu is the storyteller, the reciter, the lyrical chanter. He keeps his text before him on a lacquer reading stand, the *kendai,* although he has memorized every word. The tayu has great tonal and expressive range, and his voice can change instantly from a suggestive whisper to a howl of rage, from bass to soprano, from melody to conversational chatter. Attired in formal Japanese dress of the Edo period, seated in formal posture with legs tucked underneath him and with hands on his thighs as he starts his recitation, the tayu often rises up on his knees and gestures with his arms when the narrative reaches a crescendo. A performance by a single tayu may last from three or four minutes to as long as an hour and forty-five minutes, with infrequent silences of only seconds' duration.

A tall, handsome man dressed in a well-tailored blue suit ducks slightly as he enters the stage door of the Asahi Theatre. He smiles warmly as he greets the young musicians, cleaning women, senior puppeteers, and stagehands. The narrow corridors and low lintels of backstage make Tsudayu appear taller than his five feet nine and heavier than his one hundred sixty-five pounds. He is a large man, yet his voice seems small. His gentle speaking voice is hard to reconcile with the dramatic violence of his performances; the pleasing huskiness belies the sonority, lyric flexibility, and brisk changes in pitch that issue from the yuka when Tsudayu is narrator.

Tsudayu enters the small dressing room he shares with his son, Midoridayu, and is soon relaxing in a cotton kimono. Narrators, musicians, and puppeteers stop at his threshold to kneel and call out a greeting. He acknowledges each one pleasantly, looking each caller in the eye. Midoridayu's gaze darts around the room, checking that all is in order for his father to dress for his appearance on stage in fifteen minutes.

Tsudayu turns his head to listen closely to the words of the narrator coming from the stage over the loudspeaker. Seated, he dons a fresh pair of white *tabi* (Japanese socks). He stands up and, bowing, receives with two hands the roll of white cloth his son hands him. Tsudayu lifts it to his forehead, bows his head, closes his eyes, and moves his lips slightly in a full minute of prayer. He takes off his cotton kimono and carefully unwinds the large roll of four-inch-wide stitched linen material which he will use to encircle his trunk tightly. He strains to bind his lower abdominal area firmly, just below the hips. He then drops the rest of the roll, which unwinds on the tatami, and proceeds to wrap it less constrictingly around him. Midoridayu helps his father with the first crucial tightening of the *hara obi* (literally, "belly sash"; supporting obi) and with the final knotting and tucking. Two more layers of white undergarments go over the hara obi. Tsudayu flexes his shoulders carefully to adjust the arrangement of his crisp white kimono.

Midoridayu assists with the tying of the narrow silk outer obi after Tsudayu meticulously adjusts it just below his hips. The only sound is the flick of the stiffened gauze as Tsudayu and his son adjust the winglike vest over his shoulders, the long ends of the garment tucked into the obi front and back. Solemn and silent, he steps into the hakama his son holds open for him and, with a quick manipulation of the long belt ties, he fastens the hakama at the waist in a complicated knot.

Dropping to a kneeling position on the floor, Tsudayu uses a special clip to fasten his kimono neatly closed, and then, bowing, with both hands he receives a small green pillow from his son. He tucks it into his right sleeve and slides it across to rest above his obi in front. On his knees, he adjusts his kimono and wing-shouldered vest carefully to accommodate the bulge and then to make sure his large hands can get a full grasp on each end of this hidden bag of dried beans, the *otoshi*, used to keep his costume taut and neat.

Another formal bow greets his acceptance of a brocade case containing an amulet, which he slips into his kimono. He turns to his dressing table, runs a comb through his hair, and pats his face with a cotton towel. He looks pleasant, sober, and quite at peace. He leaves the dressing room in silence. His son follows him holding a thick book, a closed folding fan, and a covered lacquered teacup. Bowing to those who stand and voice their formal greetings, he makes his silent way upstairs, through the wings, and to the shadowy area behind the circular dais of the yuka.

Midoridayu holds out a plastic bowl of salt to his father, who takes a large pinch of it, flings it toward the dais, then claps his hands together twice, and, with hands clasped, bows his head as he silently forms the words of a long, silent prayer. He takes a small sip of hot water to moisten his throat before appearing on stage. Midoridayu is responsible for preparing the water at the exact temperature his father requires.

Kichibei, the shamisen player who will perform with him, appears, and the two men greet each other pleasantly with a phrase and a bow. They approach the revolving platform, remove their zori, and climb up to seat themselves on square floor cushions, with feet tucked beneath them in formal Japanese fashion. Tadayuki Kashiwagi, in charge of the yuka, hands Tsudayu a miniature rectangular wooden stool with a cushion attached and Tsudayu slips it between his ankles and then moves to rest his buttocks on it. He adjusts the placement of the lacquer lectern before him by an inch or two. A group of younger narrators and shamisen players who have gathered to stand in the wings near the yuka greet the pair before their performance, then watch respectfully and silently, heads bowed slightly, hands at their knees. Tsudayu repositions the bag of beans resting inside his kimono above his obi, stretches his neck, expands his chest, shifts his shoulders.

Kashiwagi and his assistant lean over the round platform, muscles taut. As the narrator on stage sings his last syllables, *"Aaaaa . . . uuuuuuu,"* the notes of the shamisen die. Tsudayu exhales, emitting a short, low "Ha." Kashiwagi immediately responds with a loud, energetic "HA!" that is echoed quickly by his assistant. With a mighty shove, the two performers who have just finished are revolved back into the wings on their half of this giant lazy susan as Tsudayu and Kichibei are whirled out into the theatre on the other half.

One hour and twenty minutes later, having narrated the concluding portion of the "Terakoya" (Village School) scene of *Sugawara Denju Tenarai Kagami,*

Tsudayu is revolved back offstage with Kichibei. The two men step from the platform, face each other, bow, and thank each other formally. Both are handed fresh towels. Tsudayu's face is covered with perspiration, and his kimono is soaked at the neck. Tsudayu smiles now, serene in his exhaustion as he makes his way, bowing and speaking small phrases of formal thanks, back to his dressing room.

The next day, Tsudayu is relaxed and hospitable as he receives the junior tayu who come to their master's home on the morning after the last day of the Osaka run to pay their respects and to express their formal appreciation for his guidance. At ease in a dark cotton kimono in the small, elegant living room of his traditional Japanese house, Tsudayu chats with his young charges and laughs often. He leans forward to listen with genuine interest, but he maintains a dignified manner befitting his role as master and an elder of the Bunraku troupe.

Tsudayu epitomizes Bunraku as an art and as a way of life. He is the embodiment of a lifetime commitment to Bunraku's traditions, the long years of disciplined training, selfless devotion, and strict adherence to a particular code of etiquette. His bearing is controlled and confident and yet his enthusiasm is evident. He often states his gratitude for the tradition he has inherited and for the obligation to impart it to his juniors.

"My father, Tsudayu III, arranged for my ceremonial debut as a tayu to take place on the sixth day of the sixth month of my sixth year," Tsudayu says, "but this was just a formality, considered very auspicious. My real debut did not take place until I was sixteen. Naturally, the sounds of Bunraku narration were part of my life from the time I was born, and my father started to train me when I was very young. I also studied with many other tayu and shamisen players. My father died in 1941. He was only sixty-two." Tsudayu gestures politely to the formal portrait of his father displayed with the memorial tablets next to the tokonoma. "Two years later, at the age of twenty-seven, I became the apprentice of Kotsubodayu II (1878–1967), whom most people now remember by his honorary title of Yamashiro no Shojo. All the tayu in Bunraku today are first or second generation apprentices of that great tayu."

Tsudayu gazes appreciatively at the small garden, thick with carefully arranged trees and shrubs, which opens directly off the end of the room. His wife, a small cheerful woman who speaks in bright Osaka accents, brings in tea and cakes. "We went to kindergarten together," Tsudayu says with a fond smile. "Who'd have thought that her father would be my master for years and that I'd marry her in the process!"

Tsudayu's wife is the daughter of the late Kanji Tsuruzawa (1887–1978), who was considered one of Bunraku's outstanding musicians. Although Tsudayu first went to Kanji to study with him, the partnership developed into a mature combination of tayu and shamisen player that was a permanent feature of Bunraku for almost a quarter of a century.

"This bookcase holds the librettos for all my performances since 1945," Tsudayu says, pointing to shelves stacked with Japanese-style books bound in soft paper. "I copy the words in my own hand, since it's really the best way to get them firmly implanted in my mind." The calligraphy is bold and round, and here and there, next to a word or syllable of the text, are marks in red that indicate intonation or tempo. "But the important thing in Bunraku narration is what is *not* written there. The tayu's art lies in bringing out what is behind the words, between the lines and in the hearts of the characters. Anyone with a decent brain can learn the words and the intonations and inflections, even the musical phrasing, but without having experienced some of life's joys and sorrows, it is impossible to portray the emotions of Bunraku. Training in breath control and studying the roles are not enough."

Pulling out the thick text he used in *Sugawara Denju*, he turns a few pages, then looks up to speak in quiet, earnest tones. "In Bunraku, the most important thing is the text. The plot, the story line, the playwright's words—these are the core of Bunraku and everyone involved must bend every effort toward creating a performance in accordance with the text. Showing off talent is not the point in Bunraku. We serve the text; the text is not to be used by performers merely to display their skills.

"If a tayu's narration is beautiful and lyrical but the audience does not understand the actual words, the narration is worthless. Similarly, if the dialogue can be understood but does not convey the character and emotions of the people involved, the tayu's words have no meaning. The tayu is not on stage as a singer, reciter, or narrator. He is there to perform a play. The playwright wrote the play for the tayu to *perform,* with the intention that puppets should also perform the play; but the tayu's performance is not merely the reading of a play, a description of action, the singing of a lament, the reproduction of a comic dialogue. The whole point of Bunraku is to portray human emotions and situations in life so that people's hearts are moved, so that they feel something special about the particular aspect of life the play deals with, whether loyalty, sacrifice, one of the many forms of love, or a dilemma one encounters in life. No, we are not mere storytellers. The tayu is the story, he is the play."

Tsudayu sits at ease; his posture is comfortably erect. "The first few decades of a tayu's training are devoted to discipline, to training his body so that he can create the voices appropriate for the roles of the play, for describing the atmosphere, for conveying certain emotions. It is only after the tayu learns to use the various parts of his body to bring forth sounds that he learns to imbue them with the proper feeling.

"Just as a flower does not bloom in order to give joy to those who behold its beauty, a tayu does not perform with the conscious intention of pleasing people in the audience. He lives to train, to accept discipline, which is the nourishment that allows him to grow. The discipline I underwent was harsh, yes, but I accept it and appreciate it because it was for my own development.

"To be able to fuse completely into the play, to become one with the words, a tayu must achieve a state of selflessness, the Buddhist *mu*. He is an empty vessel containing the play. His own feeling are set aside, he is the channel for the play itself.

"When I identify myself completely with the people in the play, I become them. The mother's grief is mine, the son's sacrifice is a part of me. When this essence flows through the mu in me, the emotions are transmitted to the people who hear the words, the melody, and the rhythm, without the interference of my own consciousness. At the end of a climactic scene in which I have been able to achieve mu, I am filled with grief or joy. Then suddenly at the end of the scene, I notice that the audience, too, feels this sadness or happiness.

"And yet," Tsudayu pauses and shakes his head thoughtfully, "at times a wave of feeling rises from the audience and envelops me in a strange way. A spark, an electric current is created between us and suddenly, unconsciously, we are all on a new level together. If I become conscious of this, the spell is broken. When I truly have mu, the play is suddenly over as if with no effort on my part. It is for those minutes that I have lived sixty-one years."

Tsudayu smiles as if to politely close a shoji on his soul. "To train the voice it is enough to learn to use the hara, the lower abdomen. That is the source, the center of both physical and spiritual strength. From the hara, the tayu's force moves up through his chest and throat, emerging from his mouth, but his posture—the position of his toes, ankles, knees, hips, shoulders, and neck—all affect the quality of the voice that emerges. A tayu learns to fill his hara with air, to extend his chest, to sit in an erect but lightly relaxed posture, to let the air out in a controlled fashion but never to center strength in the throat. The air comes from the hara through the vocal chords but it must not be forced, it must come out naturally. The throat must not be tight; the tayu must learn the *ma*—the important empty spaces, the silences, the interval between beats—and the *fushi*, the statement or melody, but these must come naturally. He trains himself to use his lips to enunciate clearly, to move his chin to give variations to the sound of the air that comes up through his throat.

"He does not, in fact, shout or whisper, imitate a woman or a man. He creates sounds that convey the essence of the femininity of a woman in love or the distillation of the rage of a vengeful man. I cannot imitate a child's voice, but what I say must sound as if a happy child speaks. How does a tayu learn this? From listening to others, from absorbing tradition, from experiencing life. A tayu is not giving a pretty concert. He is performing a play."

Tsudayu lights a cigarette and puffs at it for a minute or two. "It's funny, but when Koshijidayu and I started out as youngsters, there were thirty-six tayu our age. We are the only two left of that group. The other thirty-four spurred us on, competed with us, and the rivalry made us try harder. Perhaps it sounds unkind, but those thirty-four gave us nourishment and helped make us what we are. Competition pushes you beyond what you think are your limits. The desire to excel can only be gained from the encouragement of others, our elders and our colleagues. And when a tayu reaches the senior ranks, he wants to pass on as much as possible of what he has learned to those who are younger, who are striving for the same goal. A tayu is part of tradition, and tradition is the essence of Bunraku."

Tsudayu has the reputation of being considerate and helpful, and although his juniors confide that he is a strict and exacting teacher, he is never unreasonable, mean, or temperamental. Patient with those who demonstrate discipline and perseverance, he has little use for those who display slackness, lack of concentration or of commitment. He expects no more of others than he exacts from himself. When a film impresario once demanded that he repeat a certain sec-

24. In a lineup on an extended auxiliary stage, four tayu narrate
in chorus to the accompaniment of a group of shamisen players.

26. Koshijidayu, in silent concentration before his performance, awaits his cue before going to the yuka to narrate a scene.

5. Narrators are supported by small square stools on
e yuka, their feet carefully positioned for support also.

27. Tsudayu in prayer backstage, just before mounting the yuka.

28. Tsudayu and Danshichi perform in Osaka during a summer program. After the scene draws to its close, Tsudayu will move back within the line marking the edge of the circular stage in order to be revolved back into the wings, as the next team of tayu and shamisen player is whisked out.

29. Aioidayu and Seinosuke (in prayer) just
before being revolved out into the theatre.

30. Asazo stops to request the guidance of his master, Juzo, before appearing on the yuka during a rehearsal in the National Theatre in Tokyo.

31. Kinshi rehearses with young musicians immediately before a summer performance.

32. Taishiro Mochizuki, looking through the blinds of the geza, can keep his eye on both the stage and the yuka as he carefully coordinates his drumbeats with the action onstage.

tion of his narration, interrupting him three times to request that he start over again, Tsudayu simply said in a calm voice, "I am not a machine to be turned on and off," and walked away. No one who witnessed the scene will forget his cold, silent fury.

At dress rehearsals, Tsudayu is completely professional but cooperative towards his colleagues. A senior puppeteer interrupts the narration to request that a certain section be repeated. Tsudayu replies good-naturedly, "Yes, that exit needs more time." Only a senior puppeteer would make such a request of Tsudayu, and, even then, not without reason.

On tour Tsudayu has greetings for all, but he does not seek out the company of others, confining himself to his son Midoridayu and Kichibei, a shamisen player thirteen years his senior who is now often on the yuka with him. He does not speak of the late Kanji unless pressed to do so, for the death of a master and close colleague leaves wounds slow to heal.

"Bunraku has given me a full life," Tsudayu says, his face mirroring his sentiments. "My only regret is that I no longer get the chance to perform some of the less climactic, quieter scenes I did when I was younger. Some of them are very beautiful, others amusing and a delight to do. But in Bunraku, we older performers make way for the young ones. Progress is what keeps the Bunraku tradition alive."

Tsudayu and Koshijidayu continue as Bunraku's senior narrators. Kichibei, the shamisen player, died suddenly in 1980 at the age of seventy-seven after a short illness. Tsudayu is now usually paired on the yuka with Danshichi (formerly Danjiro), a forty-nine-year-old shamisen player. By choosing a younger musician, sixty-eight-year-old Tsudayu is following a Bunraku tradition that encourages an age disparity between pairs on the yuka to keep alive the intimate type of professional training such partnership implies; eventually Danshichi will choose a younger tayu to join him and receive from him the instruction the shamisen player earlier received first-hand from the older Tsudayu.

Shamisen Players

The shamisen player shares the yuka with the tayu, sitting to the tayu's left on a large floor cushion.

The shamisen used in Bunraku is known as the *futozao* (thick-necked) shamisen or gidayu (narrative) shamisen and is distinguished from other shamisen by its long, thick neck and its large soundbox, which gives it a resonant, masculine tone. The sonorous and deep tones of the futozao make it the bass of the shamisen family.

The three shamisen strings are of twisted silk. Cat hide is attached to both sides of the hollow wooden body; the neck, made in three jointed sections for carrying convenience, and the three long tuning pegs are also of wood. The long, heavy plectrum (*bachi*) is ivory; its blunt playing end is approximately one-quarter of an inch thick and four inches wide.

The musician plucks the strings holding the plectrum in his right hand. To achieve percussive sounds, he strikes the strings and the skinhead of the instrument in one stroke; this low guttural snap is a characteristic sound of Bunraku.

The music of Bunraku is notable for many complex changes of tempo and consists mostly of stylized motifs and mixed musical phrases, chords, or single notes commenting on the recitative sections, and occasional melodic sections of greater length used to establish atmosphere or to accompany a lament, song, or dance.

Shamisen notes include twangs, snaps, scales, and chords. The shamisen has three basic tunings, characterized in general terms as solemn, gay, or melacnholy. The player changes the tuning (*choshi*) and volume of his shamisen often during the performance by adjusting the strings at the tuning pegs and changing the bridge at the base of his instrument. The range of the shamisen is from B below middle C to B an octave above high C. In skilled hands, it has much of the expressiveness of the human voice and the versatility of a dozen types of plucked and bowed stringed instruments.

The notes of the shamisen precede or conclude action by the puppets, provide musical decoration for the tayu's words, accentuate and guide movement on stage, and increase or ease tension. The music serves to create atmosphere, underline emotion, and direct the tempo for the entire performance; it does not compete with the voice but adds punctuation and italics. When there is a silence in the narrative, the shamisen provides a musical bridge for the continuing action of the puppets. A single note appropriately struck is as important in sustaining emotion or emphasizing mood as a long melodic phrase or a rhythmic crescendo. The silences of the shamisen reinforce dramatic moments.

"A shamisen has a life of its own. Each instrument has its own personality, and the trick is to work out which shamisen is best for the musician and right for the play," says Juzo as he rests in his dressing room after a performance. He sits enfolded in a voluminous dark gray kimono, like a parcel loosely wrapped in a large piece of cloth and carefully placed on the tatami. At seventy-nine, Juzo is the oldest member of the Bunraku troupe and still an active performer in its Osaka and Tokyo performances.

"It takes a lot of playing before a shamisen reveals its character. What happens is that the player puts his own heart into the instrument, and the shamisen develops a certain tone in response."

Juzo reaches into the case by his side for his shamisen. He inserts a delicate bridge, carved of water-buffalo horn, beneath the three strings near the base of the sound box.

"I've had these bridges for about fifty years. There's no one to make good ones any more. This shamisen has a body of Chinese quince, a neck of *koki* (a type of hardwood), and pegs of black sandalwood. It's one of the five I use on stage, chosen according to the mood of the scene, the weather, and the flavor of the sound I can get out of it."

The musician places the instrument on his right knee with the casual expression of a grandfather settling down to a child, confident, happy, and relaxed.

"If someone else plays my shamisen, it just doesn't have the same tone, and similarly, if I use another's shamisen, I can get no good sounds out of it. It's really very strange. Sometimes a musician receives a shamisen from his master, but it takes a long time before he can get anything out of it at all. He simply has to make it his own. Even the finest instrument made of choice woods with catskins pasted on by the most skilled craftsman in Japan, tuning pegs perfectly aligned, and the best silk strings tied on just right—even such a shamisen will not speak until the player has spent at least thirty minutes or an hour tuning the instrument and playing it. Tuning it is not enough; it must be played. You don't just pick up a shamisen and go out on stage to play. You really have to work with it, establish a relationship with it by playing notes, passages, and melodies to get it into the proper musical condition and to bring the shamisen into harmony with yourself."

Juzo plucks the yellow strings with the heavy plectrum, the little finger of his hand tucked behind the narrow top, the three middle fingers gripping the plectrum's waist, and the thumb resting along the curve near the flaring end with which he strikes the strings. "It's the little finger that gives the strength," he says as he produces sounds that resemble the low resonant tones of a cello, the glissandos of a violin, the twangs of a plucked guitar, a sharp drum beat, the chords of a slowly bowed viola, and even a feline howl. Steady hums, scales and slides, long wavering single notes, staccato bursts, short melodies in minor keys, and lively clear motifs come from his instrument as he stares off into space and works the strings.

"A plectrum really has only three perfect days. We wind Japanese paper around the waist and paste linen down the two sides, but the flared end wears down after three performances and then it's time to trim the ivory and add a shaped wedge to fill out the flare."

Juzo glances at his young apprentice, Asazo, to make sure he is folding the master's costume properly. "Learning to play the shamisen is one thing, but learning to accompany a tayu in Bunraku is quite another matter. As a young boy, I thought the difficult part was to learn the notes and the fingering and to play a long, heavy instrument properly with an enormous plectrum for a performance lasting an hour or more. How my fingers used to ache! As I grew older, I realized that the hardest thing is to learn when *not* play, when *not* to interfere with the narration, and how to strike a single note to suit exactly the mood or emotion the tayu has established, to fit the scene or specific character at that particular point of the play. A young musician learns the notes and the beat and where his playing fits in with the tayu's words, but the most important thing is feeling, and that can only be learned in maturity."

Juzo started his musical training at the age of ten by taking koto lessons. He began his career in Bunraku by becoming the apprentice of a Bunraku musician. "Nowadays people ask about the hardships of my early training. At the time, I didn't think a thing about it. Life was that way then and young people were used to discipline, punishment, and grueling training. I used to get up early to get to my teacher's house for a lesson at six every morning. Shamisen players prided themselves on living without any heat, not even a tiny charcoal brazier, and on winter mornings it was a cold wait until my teacher was ready for me. I used to rub my numb fingers together inside the sleeves of my kimono or tuck them in the bends of my knees as I sat waiting." Juzo gives a low rumbling laugh as he bends into a gray ball, tucking his fingers beneath him as he did at his lessons sixty-seven years ago.

"And what lessons they were! My teacher would play a passage, maybe fifteen minutes long, just once. I was expected to play along with him. Next I was made to play the passage solo. My teacher would sit there scowling at me, scolding, sometimes hitting me in the face. Knowing the punishment that lay in store, I learned quickly to listen very, very carefully, straining every fiber in my body to absorb everything I possibly could with eyes, ears and mind. Oh, it was good training all right, in observation and memorizing, and since the next day's lesson was a new passage, I had to learn fast." Juzo waits for his young assistant to leave before he continues.

"In those days, our whole life was Bunraku. We had no movies, no coffee shops, no radios, no popular music to distract us. All we saw or heard was gidayu, so no extraneous sounds found their way into our ears. Our heads were full of Bunraku and only Bunraku. After my lesson and a practice session at home, I went off to spend eight or nine hours at the Bunraku theatre helping my master, doing errands, practicing, perhaps performing for a few minutes, usually hidden behind the *misu* (split-bamboo screen) that hides the young performers in a niche only they use above the regular yuka. But above all, I listened.

"In those days, the older players also listened to us young ones very con- scientiously, taking turns hearing us play and criticizing. Nowadays the youngsters depend on tapes too much, not enough on their own ears and memories. And we're not supposed to scold them, so as a result, they don't concentrate the way we had to. They expect to be taught. We learned."

Juzo's hands are large and youthful, only lightly veined, his fingers strong and slippery, the tips smooth. "The left hand has to slide up and down the neck of the shamisen," he says as he flicks a small white cloth bag into the air. It emits a puff of white powder which he rubs into his fingers. "Arrowroot powder keeps the left hand smooth. And to make sure the right hand will not slip as it grips the plectrum, we use rice-straw ash to absorb natural oils and perspiration." He picks up a few grains of the coarse gray powder and runs them through the fingers of his right hand. He grasps the plectrum and taps his nose. "Oh, yes, that little touch to the skin helps the plectrum slide over the strings. But the real secret is this." Burrowing around in his shamisen case, he brings out a small, round tin of Mentholatum. With a dab of one finger, he smears an invisible film of grease over the strings of his instrument. "In the old days, we used old-fashioned Japanese hair pomade, but it hardened in winter and was gooey in summer. One day someone discovered that this foreign medical ointment stayed the same consistency all year round. Bunraku musicians have been using Mentholatum ever since. Bunraku just couldn't survive without Mentholatum," he says, nodding seriously.

"What does it take to be a Bunraku shamisen player? The answer is easy. *Kokoro*—heart. That's all. Heart. Not strength or dexterity. Patience, yes, and perseverance to practice and practice, to repeat the same note, the same phrase over and over and over again. But without heart, the music is meaningless, the note is dead, it has no *kimochi* (feeling, emotion). Unless the feeling is conveyed, there is no point in strumming away to accompany the tayu. Our notes underline the meaning and emotions he tries to convey. Heart and feeling cannot of course be taught. Feeling can be absorbed, and the best way is to play with a good tayu. As you come to understand the feelings he conveys in his narration, feeling also intuitively colors your playing. It's impossible to explain how this happens, but suddenly you realize what love and hate and passion and revenge are all about and these feelings come out in your playing.

"In Bunraku, a musician is not a solo performer. The relationship between him and the tayu is very important, very delicate. It takes time for the right balance to be achieved. With some men, it takes weeks, years, maybe decades to achieve this empathy, but this fragile connection between the two is vital. Without it, the words and music just do not come together to give the desired effect, the flavor both seek. The two men discuss the text before they practice or perform together, but after that initial talk, the interpretation and balance they achieve must be intuitive, simultaneous. And of course it changes every day. The tayu may be strong one day, and perhaps the next day he is weaker in a certain section. I must feel it at the same time he does. I mustn't push him, I mustn't drag him, but we lend each other strength."

As Juzo speaks, he continually taps his left index finger on his shamisen case. "An old shamisen player's habit," he says. "This finger is the most precious thing a shamisen player has. I tap it to keep the tip firm, just as I did when I was a little boy. We use other fingers in playing, but it's the index finger that does most of the work." Juzo examines his finger closely. His fingernail is small and is cut very short. He wrinkles his brow seriously. "A shamisen player must never, never, put this finger in hot water. There I sit in the wooden tub, the nice hot water right up to my neck, but I tell you, I make sure that my left index finger is never in the bath water. I hold it straight up in the air. It's a mighty cold way to bathe, I assure you, but that's the way it has to be."

Juzo gets up slowly and hangs a traditional old man's purse over his wrist. He walks down the hall in small steps acknowledging the greetings of the men who stop to bow to him as he leaves, a faint aura of menthol lingering after him.

Juzo, now eighty-six, continues to give shamisen lessons at his home in Tokyo. He also attends all the Bunraku troupe's dress rehearsals in Tokyo when his former students come to him for instruction and advice after their appearances on the yuka. Juzo retired from life as a performer at a special ceremony held by the troupe at the National Theatre of Japan in Tokyo in 1980.

Offstage Musicians

The Bunraku stage is approximately forty feet wide and twenty-four feet deep; it has two levels and other special features allowing the dolls to be manipulated with ease. The two stage entrances on right and left are curtained. High over the stage-right entrance is a small room, the *geza,* in which work the three men who produce offstage musical effects.

"This is the best place in the house," says Hiroji Kineya in a fond, proprietary tone as he looks around the cramped lair he shares with the two other men who make up the geza. The bright-eyed eighty-one-year-old man in kimono turns to fill the thimble-sized bowl of his long metal pipe with a ball of wispy tobacco. "This is what keeps me going," he says, tapping his pipe, "this and a daily potion made from ground, dried snake."

"People seem to think the geza is small," says Taishiro Mochizuki, ten years Kineya's junior. His bushy white eyebrows rise and fall like those of a puppet, he nods animatedly, and his smile lights up his face. "But it's just right for the three of us. The trick is to get things laid out properly. It's hot, but we're used to the heat."

At thirty-four, Haruo Mochizuki (not related to Taishiro) is the youngest man in the offstage-music group. He studies his cue book, then peers through a split-bamboo curtain at the lighted stage.

The three men work in an area equal to a fraction more than two tatami mats, totaling six feet by six feet. The dimly lit musical nest contains five drums ranging from the size of a beer keg to an eighteen-inch hourglass; a large hanging bronze gong, which occupies one corner of the room; two small brass gongs; a selection of eighteen wooden drumsticks, some short and thick, others long and slim, paired like chopsticks; a large wooden mallet, a small one made of a slice of deer antler, and several tiny metal ones; three long-stemmed hand-bells; a pair of ridged clam shells and a large conch shell; and two silk bags bristling with bamboo flutes.

"Most people concentrate so hard on the puppets, the tayu, and the shamisen player they don't even know we're up here," Taishiro says cheerfully, "but the play would be a pretty lonely thing without us. When the atmosphere is gay, like a teahouse in the licensed quarters, our drums and flutes get everyone into a good mood, ready to enjoy themselves. When something sad is about to happen, the sound of our drums gives a warning, an ominous rolling. When there's a battle offstage, our flutes and shell trumpets and gongs and drums combine to tell you how things are going for the characters in the play."

Taishiro stands on tiptoe to look down at the stage, then picks out a flute. "This is the sad flute. The thin one has a more cheerful tone."

Near the bamboo blind, Haruo works on his small drum, the *kotsuzumi*, adjusting the tension chords on its elegantly lacquered, barbell-shaped body. By squeezing this arrangement of orange cords, Haruo controls the pitch of the drum as he hits it.

"Before I even think about tying the drum together before each performance, I have to take the weather into account. The little squares of deerskin on the inside of the front drumskin control the way the drum reverberates, and on the outside of the back I paste anywhere from one to four small squares of hand-made paper to get the right tone. It all depends on the humidity. The skin is looser in the rainy season and taut when the weather is dry, so small adjustments have to be made every day."

Haruo blows on the drumhead to soften it slightly with his breath and taps tentatively with one, then two fingers. He holds the drum lightly on his right shoulder, with his left hand clutching the tangle of chords. With the middle fingers of his right hand, he beats the end of the drum to create a variety of thumps that range from a sharp crack to a sonorous waver.

"Tuning is part of it," says Haruo, loosening the chords a bit, "but more important is knowing the feeling I want to get across when I strike. Posture is important. My stance should not be tense but I must play as if I were holding an egg securely in my right armpit."

Haruo has been playing traditional Japanese drums and gongs ever since he was a small boy, learning from his father, who is also a professional stage musician, and appearing regularly in the Bunraku geza since he was thirteen.

"The larger drum shaped like the kotsuzumi is easier to play," Haruo says, "but the problem is getting it warmed to the right temperature. We used to heat it over charcoal, but now we keep it propped up over an electric hot plate in the hallway."

As the wooden clappers on stage indicate the play is about to begin, the three men go into action. One old man blows long notes and short, brisk melodies on one flute, then several notes on another, heavier lacquered one. Haruo uses the small drum, shifting later to the larger one, which he holds over his left hip. Once the curtain opens, Taishiro stands to use slim, two-foot-long drumsticks on a large drum hide hanging from a wooden frame. He then shifts to a thin drum on a stand, hitting its twelve-inch surface with thick, short sticks. The men watch the movements of the puppets, glance at their cue books, look over at the tayu, pick up one instrument, play it, lay it down and then tackle another. They move from one piece to another with practiced precision and are as impassive as the shamisen player below them. The men occasionally call out in staccato shouts, sharp yelps, or nasal whines as they change the rhythms of their drums.

After fifteen minutes, Kineya leaves, moving carefully through the orderly clutter.

Young Haruo turns down a page in his cue book, checks his watch, and moves over to read a novel under the solitary, shaded light bulb.

Taishiro wipes the sweat from his furrowed, tanned brow, then places a damp towel on his head. "We plug up the holes in the play," he says. "People come to watch the ones out in the spotlight, but we sit up here in the shadows and help things along. That's why they call us the 'wife' of the drama. Like the woman in the dark kitchen who prepares the meals and does the housekeeping chores, people don't notice the wife unless she's not there."

He stands up to use the big drum again, and Haruo strikes the large gong with a padded mallet, stilling it after the last stroke. Kineya puffs back up the stairs. He shuffles through a drawer full of bamboo whistles. "This is the crow whistle. The cry of the evening crow is sadder and longer than that of the morning crow, so I use different whistles. I make these all myself out of the bamboo handles of writing brushes. There's one for snipe cries, another for crickets, several for other crying insects. Then there are the nightingale whistle, the plover, the owl, and various water birds. The rooster is the same whistle as the one for the crying baby. Ghosts are hard to do because I've never heard one," he chortles.

Haruo now works on the drum propped on a stand. "This takes about ten minutes of hard work to tie together. It's difficult to play the different drums because there are so many effects they can convey. There's water for instance— one tempo for a small, softly flowing stream, another for a rushing river. For snow, there are sounds for delicate flurries and dull persistent beats with a single padded drumstick for the dreaded heavy snow. Waves can be gentle ones that lap the shore or enormous ones of a storm creating havoc in a battle at sea. It's important to convey in the drumbeat just the right feeling the words should evoke. Mood is vital in Bunraku. Our music helps the puppeteers and also adds another dimension to what the tayu creates with his words and the musician with his shamisen. We're not competing with them, we're filling out the empty corners, underlining plot lines, intensifying emotions. We don't want to call attention to ourselves, we just want to make the play a more moving and entertaining experience. We don't try to make fake sounds or truly realistic imitations. The important thing is to create effects that make the audience recall an emotion or an experience."

As a professional classical drummer, Haruo takes pride in meeting the various challenges of the theatre. "Balance is what counts. The puppeteers like our musical effects to be precise, rather loud, and timed perfectly with their movements. We must not challenge the tayu, not overpower the emotions he conveys. Similarly, we must not interrupt the music of the shamisen player. The balancing of all these factors is what keeps me tense. The puppeteer wants the drum to come in earlier, faster, but the tayu doesn't want to have his rhythm thrown off. The shamisen player will be distracted if the flute cuts off his important twang. The effect of the throb of the shamisen skin when struck with the plectrum would be ruined by too obtrusive a drumbeat.

"I have my own cue books, twenty-three years' worth, but we often make changes as requested by a performer. We never know about these until we come to the dress rehearsal, where all the elements of a Bunraku play first come together."

During a scene in which there is a great deal of dialogue, the geza remains deserted for as long as thirty minutes. One of the trio may climb up to strike a few notes on a bell or to beat a drum and then disappear downstairs again.

The busiest times are just before the curtain opens and just as it closes. "We work to create the mood of anticipation before the play starts, blending our music, usually drumbeats, occasionally some flute passages, with the sound of the wooden clappers sounded in the wings," Haruo says. "At the end, we must leave people with a feeling about the play that they take home with them."

During quiet spells in their cranny, Taishiro and Kineya chat about the old days, recalling forgotten drumbeats or a bell rung too early. "Oh yes, the puppeteers get mad, but we cover up for their mistakes often enough so it all comes out even," says one.

"One thing's different nowadays," says another. "In the old days the puppeteers often used to thank us for our efforts. Monjuro often did that. That really brings some light into these shadows. I like to remember his words when things get hectic up here." His eyes mist over for a few seconds.

The two old men put aside their tobacco and stand poised, nerves and muscles tensed with feline concentration to pounce upon the next section of musical effects. The young man blows on his drum. *"I-i-i-i, ya!"* he calls out.

Kineya has retired but Taishiro Mochizuki, now seventy-eight, and Haruo Mochizuki, forty-one, continue their performances in the geza, assisted by one or two other musicians who regularly join them in Tokyo or Osaka. Although they say their new lair is cooler, an electric fan is necessary for comfort and tuning the drums is complex because of the lack of humidity attributable to the air conditioning. The musician who specializes in flutes carefully wraps his ten instruments in their silk case and takes them home after each performance. Taishiro confides that he works in Western dress during rehearsals but feels that his music sounds better when he is attired for performances in kimono.

Selection of Heads

The distributor of heads (*kashirawari iin*) assigns puppet heads (kashira) to the chief puppeteers for their roles in puppet plays.

Upstairs, senior puppeteer Bunjaku peers into a storage drawer full of puppet heads. As distributor of heads, it is his job to select the ones that will best fit the character of each role. The troupe owns close to 300 heads and several leading puppeteers have their own which they sometimes prefer to use on stage in certain roles. Bunjaku is familiar with the line of the chin, the length of the nose, the furrows of the brow, and the cheek line of every kashira.

"I have a mental inventory so I can shuffle this information around in my head and come up with the appropriate kashira for each part." The puppeteer's round face breaks into a smile. "It's all in there," he says, pointing to his graying temples. "I have to be a computer."

The Bunraku Association and the National Theatres of Tokyo and Osaka consult with master puppeteers Tamao and Kanjuro and with leading narrators Tsudayu and Koshijidayu to reach a decision on plays to be performed, to assign roles to the puppeteers in the troupe, and to apportion scenes or parts thereof to tayu and musicians. It is then up to Bunjaku to choose the head for each role.

There are roughly forty different types of heads in general use in Bunraku today and about thirty special ones. The puppet heads fall into natural categories: male and female; young, old, and middle-aged; good and evil—each with its refinements.

Behind the locked sliding doors of the kashira closet in the theatre in Osaka twenty-one large wooden boxes fill shelves arranged from floor to ceiling. In the carton marked "Young woman" (*musume*) in Japanese characters are seven heads that vary only slightly in detail. All the faces are of white complexion, youthful and pretty. Some eyes are bright and small, others large; some cheeks are plump, some more delicately molded. The lips of one young woman look as if they were about to part to utter something tender. The mouth of another looks less girlish, the chin less rounded.

Middle-aged women (*fukeoyama*) are in the box below, and the heads lying in it display a quality of maturity not found in the sweet and lovely innocence of the young-woman heads. Even as the heads lie here in storage, the fukeoyama convey the settled, determined character of married women imbued with a loyalty, devotion, and intelligence. In contrast, the heads in the courtesan (*keisei*) box radiate the allure and sensuality of the highest ranking prostitutes, *oiran* of the licensed quarters of the Edo period. "For a lower ranking woman of the gay quarters, like most of the courtesans who commit suicide with their lovers in Chikamatsu's plays, we often use a particularly beautiful and sensual young-woman head and give her a courtesan's hairdo," Bunjaku says.

Sharp chins, puckered lips, and lined brows distinguish the heads used for wicked old women from those destined for the roles of understanding, kindly grandmothers in the box marked "Old Woman" (*baba*). The heads used for elderly court ladies and statesmen's wives have a decidedly patrician quality, which the shopkeepers' mothers lack.

"Genta," the name of a young warrior in a historical play, is the identifying label on another box. It contains a dozen puppet heads depicting older boys (*waka otoko*) and young, handsome men. The Genta and waka-otoko heads are all pale, good looking, and youthful, but there is a tragic weakness in the mouth line of most, and a definitely seductive attractiveness in others. Restraint, good intentions, and innocence glow here, but there are also expressions of impatience, perhaps indulgence—that look of a playboy or a youth destined for tragedy or disaster.

The Komei box contains male heads marked by an air of maturity and complexity. Wisdom, strength, and refinement, perhaps an undertone of regret, are sculpted into these flesh-colored faces. One particularly handsome Komei kashira seems heavy with sorrow, or is it merely sober reflection or nostalgia?

The next box is filled with dark-complexioned, even ugly faces. These middle-aged villains, crooks, and bullies have round eyes, rather than the almond-shaped eyes of the noble characters. Greed and violence distort these visages, which are larger than the heads of men of nobler sentiment that occupy a drawer labeled "Kembishi." The Kembishi heads have many variations, too, but share an air of integrity, strength, intelligence, and sorrow. Yet another box holds heads used for men who have a base streak but who cannot be classified as villains; these heads, painted a light beige, present varying ratios of good and bad qualities.

The most important puppet head in Bunraku and the most majestic head of all, Bunshichi, comes in some seven variations and occupies an entire box. Whether it is the regular or the large-sized head, the specially coiffed or the scarred, the Bunshichi head conveys tested strength of character and iron will tinged with grief. The heads are marked by masculinity and determination, but the heavy brows and strong, downturned mouths reflect tragic emotions masked by the courage and determination typical of a samurai true to his code of honor.

"Old Man" (*ojii*) is the marking on a box in the middle tier. A dozen heads crowd the box, good faces mix with bad, kindly with cruel, sympathetic and pathetic with greedy and violent. The standard father head looks far less severe than the one classified "father-in-law." The unaffected loyalty of a kindly old man of the countryside contrasts sharply with the cruelty delineated in the white face of an upper-class tyrant. Old-man heads are much used, and the contents of the box make clear the subtleties of character differentiation.

Other boxes contain puppet heads for comic characters, fools, ghosts, and harmless warriors. Happy-go-lucky maids or country wives, a pugnacious man of good humor, a ferocious-looking man who is in the end revealed to be a good samurai despite his frightening mien—these types for supporting roles of mixed good and evil are stored together. Heads used for children, boys and girls of tender ages, some ordinary, some definitely aristocratic, are lined up in another box. Special heads used only for one particular role occupy still another box. The tsume, the one-man puppets used for the walk-on parts of serving girls, ladies-in-waiting, palanquin bearers, messengers, farmers, constables, and urban bystanders are divided into two boxes by sex. Their faces are cheerful, often comic, simple and artless.

Bunjaku knows each puppet head. He discusses the cruelty of one, the hard life of another, the streak of humor in another, as if he were talking of friends or acquaintances.

"There's lots to keep in mind even for well-known roles. For instance, a puppeteer will have a personal preference for a certain type of head—some puppeteers always choose young-woman heads with big eyes or a particularly sensuous Genta. Even more important, however, is their style of manipulation. Each puppeteer uses the kashira and moves the doll a little differently. Why? Well, in the first place their hands are different sizes: some have long fingers, some short; some have strong, large fingers, others have surprisingly small fingers; palms are all different. The sensitivity of the puppeteers' hands varies remarkably. The tension they maintain while holding the headgrip, and the special fingering they devise to achieve certain effects with the puppet heads differ tremendously and affect how the doll comes across on stage.

"The headgrips, which are permanently attached to the kashira and thus of course not interchangeable, fit into one hand one way, but another chap may tilt or twist the headgrip quite differently to turn the head or to lower the chin. Expression is achieved by raising or lowering the head to look downward or upward and by tilting the headgrip at the same time to change the angle of the head."

Bunjaku reaches for a Bunshichi head and fingers the headgrip, gripping it firmly. "What it means is that the way we hold the headgrip greatly influences the way the puppet head succeeds in conveying character and emotions. It's not only what shows—the modeling of the head itself, the firm chin, the bright eyes, the thin cheeks, the weak mouth—but also what the audience can't see—the unseen fingering of the headgrip and its toggles."

Bunjaku is responsible for matching the skills and personality of the puppeteer to the puppet head appropriate for the part. "I have to consider the puppeteer's tastes, style, idiosyncrasies, and skill as well as the way he wants to play the role: what complexities does he want to emphasize—the abandoned wife's loneliness, say, or her loyalty to her husband?" As an experienced puppeteer who plays many leading female roles and, occasionally, male ones also, Bunjaku brings his long experience as a performer to bear on his responsibility of suiting the kashira to the role.

The composition of the program must be noted. "One long play such as

Sugawara Denju may call for five variations of the Bunshichi head, since the emotions expressed in different scenes need different mouth lines or face sizes. Or, a role may be played with a Genta head in one scene, but by the more mature Kembishi head later on, as in *Kanadehon Chushingura*. If the program is made up of scenes from several different plays, young women are apt to appear in two or even four of them, so I choose different musume heads to make the program interesting."

In 1963, when the great puppeteer Bungoro died in his nineties, the troupe elected Bunjaku, one of Bungoro's senior apprentices, to the job of head distributor. "I'd been with Bungoro for twelve years and had had a hand in selecting heads during much of that time, and, even before that, with my previous master, Tamaichi.

"The only difficulties that crop up come when we do a revival of a play not done for a century or so, or when we do a new play. For the old plays, there are few written records, and we're on completely new ground with an original play, so the first thing I have to do is to study the text very, very carefully."

With lists and notebook in one hand and a bundle of wispy paper tags in another, Bunjaku starts his job of choosing the heads that will be used in the troupe's next two months of performances. Hishida, guardian of the twenty-one storage boxes and the man responsible for keeping the kashira in repair, assists him.

Looking at the Bunshichi box, Bunjaku points to two of the heads. Hishida picks one up and attaches a small slip of filmy paper reading "Matsuo/tour/Tamao" to the string of the main toggle, identifying the role, performance and doll operator. In less than an hour, the two men work through the list, scene by scene, for a Shikoku tour. The next afternoon Bunjaku works to assign heads for the next Tokyo run. Close to one hundred kashira for three-man puppets as well as scores of tsume heads are tagged or listed for thirteen plays.

"It's like a big chess game that never ends," Bunjaku says. "The choice of puppet heads sometimes even determines the character of the shamisen music; additionally, the tayu bases his tone and style on the personality conveyed by the particular head that is chosen. So you can really say that the entire temper of the play rests on the selection of the heads."

Puppet heads are stored in the new Osaka theatre, in the boxes brought there from the Asahi-za, in the room shared by the wig master and the repairer of heads.

Among the photographs in this book are some taken at rehearsals and performances of *Sugawara Denju* (May 1983, National Theatre of Japan, Tokyo) and *Sonezaki Shinju* (February 1984, Tokyo; July 1984, National Bunraku Theatre, Osaka). The kashira used for these performances were as follows:

For the "Terakoya" scene of *Sugawara Denju:*

Tonami, wife of Genzo	fukeoyama
Genzo, the schoolmaster, loyal to Sugawara	Kembishi
Kanshusai, Sugawara's son	male child (large)
other students	tsume (children)
Chiyo, wife of Matsuomaru	fukeoyama
Kotaro, her son	male child
Matsuomaru, father of Kotaro, secretly loyal to Sugawara	Bunshichi
Gemba, retainer of the minister demanding Kanshusai's head	Kintoki
fathers, grandfathers	tsume (male)
Kanshusai's mother	fukeoyama

For *Sonezaki Shinju:*

Tokubei, the clerk in love with Ohatsu	Genta
Chozo, his apprentice	Dechi
Ohatsu, a courtesan	young woman (musume)
Kuheiji, Tokubei's rival	Darasuke
other courtesans	young woman
proprietor	hayaku
Otama, the comic maid	Ofuku
bystanders	tsume (male)

Carver of Heads

The head (kashira) of a Bunraku doll is hand-carved of Japanese cypress (*hinoki*), painted white, pink, or beige and permanently attached to a headgrip, which is inserted into the framework of the doll's body. A head measures from three to four inches wide by three to five and one-half inches high. With only half a dozen exceptions, every one of the almost 280 puppet heads used in Bunraku performances today is the work of Minosuke Oe, the seventy-year-old carver of wood who works in a village not far from Naruto on the island of Shikoku. Oe also makes the wooden arms, hands, legs, and feet of the puppets.

Minosuke Oe sits in the back row of the Asahi Theatre watching the Bunraku performance with a smile, nodding and cocking his head, taking measure of his creations.

After a few hours in the theatre, he joins the wig master and keeper of heads in their workroom upstairs to deliver one new puppet head and two that he has repaired and completely refinished, and to turn over several pairs of hands and legs to individual puppeteers.

"That *Hiragana Seisuiki* (Chronicles of Decline and Prosperity) that's going on downstairs is the first Bunraku play I ever saw," Oe says, running his fingers through his white hair. "In 1930, to celebrate my recovery from a lung ailment that had kept me in bed at home for five years, I came up to the old Bunraku-za in Osaka and saw that great play about the Heike-Genji struggles. I remember it very clearly because I was fascinated.

"I was only twenty-three, but, since my grandfather had carved puppet heads, I was introduced to the great puppeteer Monzo. He knew that I'd helped my grandfather carving *oshishi* (mythical lion) heads so he persuaded me to repair puppet heads. Before I knew it, I'd fixed up fifty heads." Oe laughs. "Yes, that was the beginning—*Hiragana Seisuiki*."

Oe leans back against the shelves behind him. He points to a Yokambei head hanging in one of the notched lengths of bamboo in the head room. "One of the first heads I carved on my own was a Yokambei for Tamazo, father of today's Tamamatsu," Oe remarks, "but the very first kashira of mine that was used on stage was the Genta head for puppeteer Bungoro in 1932. I was busy carving after that, and Bungoro really kept after me. He said I led too virtuous a life to be able to carve a properly seductive female puppet head. He kept telling me that I should take up sakè and women. Well, I never did, but my carving improved, and in later years he would tell me that my young-woman heads were to his liking. He was a great tease, that Bungoro, right up until the end."

Oe came to know members of the Bunraku troupe well during the eight years he spent in Osaka. He learned their performing styles, their hand sizes, their tastes in kashira and handgrips. Even more important, he became familiar with the plays in the Bunraku repertory, most of which are still performed and to which only a handful of new pieces have since been added.

In 1938, Oe decided it was time to return home to Shikoku to devote his energies to carving kashira full time, limiting his visits to the theatre to a day or two during Osaka and Tokyo runs or when the troupe toured Shikoku.

This handsome man in the gray beret, with his jacket buttoned closed even in hot weather, is a familiar sight to early risers in Oshiro Otsu, his home town in Tokushima Prefecture. Soon after sunup, Oe rises, lets out his white cat and brews himself a cup of tea. He then walks briskly along narrow village roads and past muddy fields shoulder-high in greenery: huge round lotus leaves shading their pointed pink blossoms. He often continues up into the hills latticed with bamboo scaffolding set around pear trees heavy with paper-clad fruit. After a leisurely breakfast with his wife, Oe goes into his workshop a few minutes after eight.

He seats himself at a low desk. Casually brushing aside an inkstick and a small inkstone, several brushes, a handful of chisels, and two half-finished puppet heads, he picks up a sheaf of simple front-face sketches. He drops the papers absentmindedly and picks up a partially carved male kashira. Holding it lightly, he studies it intently, tilting it this way and that. The morning light creates shifting shadows and changing features as Oe rocks the sculpted wooden oval in his hand.

Oe sits cross-legged and steadies one knee against a large, scarred, low workblock of pinewood. Using a knife with a small triangular blade, he starts to carve below the lip line with short strokes. The knife makes a soft sound as it cuts into the wood. The only other sound is Oe's rhythmic breathing as he blows away the tiny shavings onto the tatami. The air is fragrant with the aroma of Japanese cypress. "For female dolls, the lips are a key to character. But all features are important, for both male and female dolls. Even the contours of the ears can convey a great deal."

Oe sets the kashira aside, and his lined face breaks into a smile. "This Kembishi-type head is difficult, you know. He's got to be a good-looking chap but not sensual, strong but stubborn. He's used for Choemon, the obi merchant in *Katsuragawa* and for Genzo, the schoolmaster in *Sugawara Denju* so he must be handsome but without outward seductive attractiveness. I want to get across his maturity, and he must be gentle but with inner strength. When I carve a kashira, I think of the various plays in which that particular head appears, analyze the character, and put those thoughts into the way I use my tools."

He puts the Kembishi down and finds a Darasuke. "Now this man is a tough one. People think of Darasuke as evil but that is wrong." Tapping his head with a chisel for emphasis, Oe goes on. "In Darasuke I want to create a man who is a bit rough, inconsiderate, sometimes base, but not completely evil. Think of Kuheiji in *Sonezaki Shinju*. He's a Darasuke: not an out-and-out villain, but he has a nasty streak. This must show in his face."

Hinoki wood from the famous cypress forests of Kiso in central Japan is what Oe uses for all puppet heads except the simple tsume heads manipulated by single puppeteers which are made of *kiri* (paulownia). "I bought enough Kiso hinoki years ago to last me a lifetime, I thought, but I've been healthier than expected so I had to order some more—from Nara, this time. Never expected to be still carving, what with the problems I've had breathing all my life."

Oe reaches behind him and, with a grunt of effort, pulls out a thick, cleft wedge of cypress. He becomes silent as he measures carefully with a variety of rules and squares. He marks the wood in several places, stops to search for his glasses, and continues to measure, turning the cypress this way and that, then turning it over to repeat the meticulous markings on the reverse side.

"A sculptor is probably not as fussy about measuring," Oe says cheerfully, "but since my pieces will be used on headgrips by puppeteers operating from the back, the line from the top of the head down through the neck is very important. It must be absolutely straight or the head will never look erect."

With a hatchet that seems dangerously large for the size of the block he is tackling, Oe chops at the wedge to roughly form the oblong core he has outlined. He then works with a long double-edged saw along the sides. A moment later, he enlists his wife to swing a wooden mallet down onto the back of a still larger hatchet, while he controls the angle of the blade. He cleaves off long splinters and shapes the block.

"I get my wife to do a lot of the hard work these days," says Oe with a grin. His wife gives a good-natured laugh and takes over the hatchet work.

"He lets me do things that take strength," she says between blows. "I only started carving puppet heads four or five years ago. When my husband was out, I'd practice with his tools, trying to remember everything I'd seen him do. One day I worked up my courage to substitute a head I'd carved all by myself for a kashira he'd almost finished. He didn't notice it at first, but when he did, he said it wasn't bad. I've been helping him ever since."

Oe glances at his wife with a sternly affectionate look. "Yes, she's learned enough to take over many of the first stages. Well, that's it. A bit off here. And then plane it down for me, will you?" Mrs. Oe pulls a large plane over the roughly cylindrical piece of cypress. She turns it, planes all sides, and then hands it cautiously to her husband. He nods. She starts to smile, then turns serious and leaves the room with a handful of cypress curls.

Oe takes a pencil to mark in the central nose line, the intersecting eye line, and the mouth line. He brushes in outlines of the features with *sumi* ink and, working quickly now, picks up a chisel and gouges out large splints of wood. He gradually decreases the size of his tools, and the size of the chips reflect this. Within forty minutes from the time he slides the cypress slab onto his workblock, the features of the kashira have taken shape.

After a pause for cup of tea, a chat with his cat, and a lively reminiscence with his wife about the ways of puppeteers of the past, Oe returns to his work refreshed. He selects a puppet head whose carving is almost complete. "A little more here around the ears," he says. He calls for his wife again to wield the mallet as before, this time to split the completed head in two, front and back. Satisfied at the way the head is divided, the pieces rocking like hard-boiled egg halves on a picnic table, he hums as he fits the two parts together again, nods, and then shoves them aside to be hollowed out later.

Using a tool with a U-shaped blade, Oe works on the inside of still another kashira until it resembles a thin mask, finishing the edges of almost almond-shaped holes into which eyeballs will be fitted. He measures silk strings and bits of black whalebone. "The baleen (*kujira no hige,* literally, "whale's beard") is the secret of the realistic movements of the eyes, mouths, and heads in Bun-raku. A narrow strip of strong, flexible baleen functions as a spring to make the eyes close smoothly rather than jerk shut and the head to lower naturally instead of drop."

A headgrip on the floor distracts Oe and he picks it up to whittle at it. "This headgrip has to fit into the shoulder board without slipping about, has to be right for the puppeteer's hand and balanced for the weight of the head, so this little stick, cut from local cypress, is very important. The neck is attached to the headgrip at an angle, tilted more for a female doll, and a long baleen spring attached inside the neck is fastened to the inside of the head."

Into two other holes in the top of the carved head, an old shamisen string is attached, then brought down the neck into a channel cut in front of the head-grip and tied to the main toggle, the *choi.* This wooden toggle controls the most important movements of the head, the up-and-down or nodding move-ment basic to all expressions. The baleen spring works to keep this head action smooth.

"The heavy silk threads that operate the eyes, mouth, and brows come down into little channels at the back of the neck and continue down the back of the headgrip. Small toggles *(kozaru)* are attached. The puppeteer grasps the headgrip with his left hand, the main toggle between his middle and ring fingers, and he moves his thumb to control the small toggles in the back of the headgrip. It sounds complicated," he says with a dry laugh, "but it's all very neatly worked out. It takes careful threading and adjustment to get the cords and baleen the right length. Those whale-beard strips—they're the secret. I often wonder who ever thought of using baleen. Really very clever."

Once the two halves have been carved out and the mechanisms inserted, the hollowed-out puppet head is glued back together and given as many as twelve coatings of different grades of *gofun*, a type of gesso made of ground seashells and glue. If the drying is too fast, the gofun will shrink and crack, so timing and temperature control are critical. White, beige, or a deep pink is used for the face, and Oe also paints in the lines to accentuate eyes, noses, or jowls.

Final assembly of the finished head onto its neck and then onto the headgrip, with all the intricate knotting of silk cords through carved channels and into tiny toggles, is a delicate job. Oe's reward is the special moment of recognition when he holds the finished kashira. Operating the big toggle in the front of the headgrip and the tiny toggles in the back, he creates the expression he wants. "Yes, that's a Kembishi, all right. No doubt about what kind of man he is."

Oe spends as much effort and care in carving hands, joining finger joints, tying together a leg at the knee, and painting calves and thighs of paulownia wood as he does in making heads. "It's not quite so demanding creatively, so I often do heads in the morning and then arms and legs in the afternoon. Carving, hollowing out, and inserting the string mechanism all take time, but the most important part is the contours. The curve of the thumb, the size of the calves, these details are important in conveying character in keeping with the type of head. A droopy thumb shows weakness, beautifully carved fingers can be sensual, scrawny legs indicate age."

Oe's pleasant face turns serious. "This is not sculpture for decoration. I think out the roles for each head, each finger, each eye, each toe, each nose I carve. The play's the thing. A kashira portrays character. The headgrip I carve allows the puppeteer to show his artistry. It is my link with his heart. In Bunraku, the play's the thing. The puppeteer and I work independently to bring it alive together. I carve. He moves. But it's the play that counts."

Minosuke Oe, now seventy-seven, and his wife spend their days working together on kashira, seldom making limbs these days. Mrs. Oe makes the toggles her husband requires. Hishida, the troupe's head repairer, visits frequently for guidance and instruction; he carves limbs, new tsume heads, and occasionally a kashira. Oe worked with youthful excitement putting the finishing touches on a Yasuna head of paulownia for the 1984 performances of *Ashiya Doman Ouchi Kagami,* since he was eager to recreate the important kashira he made fifty-one years ago which had been destroyed during the war. "I must admit, paulownia wood is easier to work with than the denser Japanese cypress now that rheumatism in my arms occasionally flares up," he confided.

Wig Master

The wig master is in charge of all hairdressing, the making and attaching of wigs, and the changing and dressing of all coiffures for the puppet heads the Bunraku troupe uses.

Seated cross-legged on a disorderly stack of floor cushions in the workroom he shares with the keeper of the heads, wig master Shoji Nakoshi peers over his thick glasses as senior puppeteer Bunjaku enters. He drops the long-handled wooden comb he has been using to smooth the intricate coiffure of the courtesan head clamped into the low bamboo stand in front of him and reaches out to receive one of the puppet heads for the next program.

"Every time I think I'm getting caught up with the lists, in come more heads," Nakoshi says with a wry laugh. He rises, spilling forth scissors, a hammer, tacks, balls of black hair, a lustrous chignon, and a colorful hairpin from his lap. They fall unnoticed into the chaos of hairpieces, ribbons, and bald wooden pates that surround him.

Nakoshi and Bunjaku place the heads selected for the next play on the few bare surfaces left in the room—a length of empty shelving, the corner of a desk piled high with books and boxes, several square, papered baskets, and layers of newspaper spread over the tatami floor. Bamboo toggles on the headgrips click and clatter.

From notched lengths of thick bamboo, thirty-five kashira hang motionless, their headgrips inserted in neat triangular gashes. Tin boxes overflow onto the floor with bits of topknots and forelocks and underpinnings of matted balls of hair. Bottles of lacquer, a can of hairspray, heaped ashtrays, pinch-type Japanese scissors tangled into the handles of tailor's shears, writing brushes and wooden combs, an electric hair dryer, tweezers, needles, and bunches of hair litter Nakoshi's section of the room.

The way the hair is dressed conveys to a Bunraku audience not only the sex, age, and social position of the role portrayed but also the occupation and, in the case of females, marital status. The hairdo on a kashira also indicates whether the character is good or bad, rustic or urban, in court, religious, or military life, calm or distraught, and a figure in a historical tale or a drama about ordinary folk.

"I've got about a hundred hairdos in my head, but I have to consult my notes for the others," Nakoshi says. "All the coiffures are the ones people actually wore in the Edo period, or as recreated by us according to what we know about those days. Even stories taking place in the tenth century like *Sugawara Denju* are set, as far as hairdos and costumes go, in the middle of the Edo period, about 1750. Hairdressing was very complicated, and every little curve in a topknot or chignon, even the puff of a sidelock, told something about the wearer. An Osaka merchant tied his hair one way, a southern samurai another, a daimyo quite differently, and an Edo shopkeeper quite differently again."

Styles of Edo-period topknots had names like "mushroom," "chestnut burr," "tea whisk," and "hundred-days' growth," and there were sidelocks that stood out from the face like wide-toothed combs, in braids, or drawn into bouffant semicircles. A young unmarried woman wore a certain style of hair ornament, a courtesan quite another. The wife of a samurai would never be mistaken for a fisherman's wife because the hairdos were so distinctive, and a merchant's daughter would be coiffed differently from a country girl.

After receiving puppet heads from Bunjaku, the troupe's distributor of heads, or other puppeteers after the end of a play's run, Nakoshi removes old wigs, rearranges or re-dresses attached hairpieces, and makes new coiffures by assembling wig parts and shaping new arrangements. Although he often uses various old parts of wigs from his remarkable jumble of supplies, many hairdos Nakoshi creates hair by hair in the traditional way.

"The hair styles for the main roles in standard plays are easy to remember. I refer to my notes for special topknots for supporting roles, the curve of the sidelocks in rarely done plays, or the piles and knots that some of the female arrangements require. I know exactly what bits and pieces I have here. It may take me a while to dig out the part I want, but if I rummage around long enough, I can always find it."

Nakoshi works calmly but always seems to be doing several things at once. He shapes the pyramid of buns and knots on the head of a courtesan doll. To create a bit of bright cording that the courtesan's intricate coiffure needs, he bastes a strip of silk to the tip of his left sock. A few minutes of careful stitching, maintaining tension on the end of the anchored strip with his arched toe, and it's finished. He removes the colorful puppet head from the stand in front of him and slips it by its headgrip into an empty slot in the bamboo head rack behind him.

After settling an antique wooden stand firmly in front of him, Nakoshi attaches a paper-wrapped bunch of hair as thick as a broccoli stalk to the middle crosspiece. He reaches in to pull the entire black tuft partially out of the paper and pinches a few hairs between his thumb and forefinger, extracting them neatly in one pull. With a quick gesture he delicately loops the tiny bunch around two silk threads strung across the top of the stand.

"A Japanese straw rain cape or *mino* is woven in much the same way and that's why we call this fringe a mino. Strips of rice straw are woven together only at the collar to make a raincoat that is really a loose cascade of straw. I just tie one small bunch of hair after another onto these two threads to make a long, thin fringe of hair. This mino is for the very front of the coiffure, so I'm only looping on fifteen hairs at a time. Hair that is used underneath is tied on in bunches of forty or one hundred. Now and then I have bets with the puppeteers about how accurate I am in pulling out exactly twenty or forty hairs at a time for these mino. I win nine times out of ten. After twenty years, my fingers know," Nakoshi says laughing, but then turns serious.

"This is hard on the eyes, this mino business. But there's something even worse." Nakoshi pushes away the mino stand and brings out another battered stand that resembles a wig block. "This is a beard, and I'm attaching the hairs one by one to a base of silk net. Some of the wigs are made that way too, one hair at a time attached to silk material. But for most wigs, it's the mino stand."

Nakoshi uses human hair for mino in lengths of ten to twenty inches. "It used to be Japanese hair, but now, what with permanents and hair dyes, we have to use hair imported from China, Korea, and Thailand. I use a lot of yak hair too (from Tibet) but not in the mino. Yak hair is soft and fine and strongly resembles human hair."

Dropping the bent crochet hook he uses for the single-hair weaving process, Nakoshi reaches behind him once again and beams with delight at his find. "Yup, it's a yak tail. A man here in Osaka brought it to me. A Sherpa gave it to him. He heard on some television program about Bunraku that we use yak hair, and the next day he turned up with the tail. Very handy, too. Nice soft, long hair."

Nakoshi pushes aside the beard stand and rummages around to pull out a small square of copper sheeting. He hums as he measures and picks up a bald female kashira identifiable by its painted black head with a peg protruding from the top. Using a paper pattern of the curve and size of the bare puppet head, he cuts the copper into a strip then beats it to create a curved headband. A puppeteer interrupts him to request a special knot for the wig for a kashira he will be using in a future program. Nakoshi makes a scribbled note, then turns to one of his many stands to comb, knot, and pound.

He sews a length of a mino fringe into perforations in a copper headband and nails two such bands to a bare kashira. The neck hair, side lengths, and various layers of hair from the forehead are knotted, looped, stuffed, and tied into place with fine paper string. Nakoshi uses his fingers delicately, and he tightens many knots by holding one end of the paper string in his right hand, firming the tie with his left index finger, and holding the other end of the string between his teeth. "Could never do Bunraku hairdressing without both hands, both feet, a good set of teeth, and thick glasses," he mumbles.

To create the attractive loops and curves so typical of both male and female hairdos of the Edo period, Nakoshi uses several varieties of wax, one a special old mixture, called *bintsuke*, that hardens to create durable topknots. The heat of a small electric hair dryer brings out the sheen in some sidelocks attached to a male puppet head; a squirt or two of hair spray keeps a married woman's coiffure neat and lustrous.

"Those complicated hairdos the top-class courtesans wear, with all their combs and baubles, aren't as hard as they look. What's harder is balding old men. The hairstyles of military figures are difficult to create too, and some of those topknots drive me crazy—hard to shape properly at the neck, then pull over and loop on top of the head and tie neatly. I can't use hair oil on the puppets' hair as human beings do—it ruins the painted finish of the kashira.

"But the hardest of all, believe it or not, are the hairdos for young emperors, princesses, or elderly nobles that are just gathered at the back in a strip of silk or binding cord. They have to hang just right, but they mustn't get caught in the neckline of the kimono. The weight has to be worked out so that the puppeteer can still tilt and nod the doll's head properly."

In scenes of grief, passion, action in battle, suicide, and murder, hair is loosened for dramatic or realistic effect. A few loose strands of hair at the temples add an air of erotic abandon to a young male or female doll; a whole head of loose hair indicates a samurai's frenzied efforts in hand-to-hand combat; and a fall of all the back hair adds passion to a courtesan's frantic dance-prayer for ransom money. "When the hairdo comes tumbling down on stage, during a *seppuku* scene or a fight scene, it means that the puppet head has to be brought up to me again to be re-dressed for the next performance. Some programs have lots of those scenes; it's a damnable job retying all those trick strings.

"The hardest thing about my work is to get the wig attached properly in the first place. The copper base must be nailed firmly to the wooden head, the lengths of hair have to be tied and anchored strongly. The puppets move around at a great rate, so the hairdo has to be secure. I don't want stuffing dropping out or knots loosening. And of course it has to look nice. But even more important than looking attractive, the hairdo has to fit the role exactly. It has to express character as well as position. Why, a wig can change a stern samurai into a genial country gentleman or can show that the fisherman is really an important court official in hiding."

Nakoshi has spent twenty-five years at his craft. "Easier than my parents' work. They do human beings' hair. At least the dolls don't complain. And every new hairdo is a challenge. I watch the plays for a bit now and then to make sure the hair looks right, but I never have time to see the whole thing."

Nakoshi radiates a quiet contentment. He has the confident modesty and devotion to his work typical of the true Japanese craftsman. He keeps calm under the pressures of complicated schedules, exacting puppeteers, changing programs, and the lack of an assistant. "As long as my eyes hold out, I reckon I can keep at this. But without an assistant to carry on later . . . " He sighs, then shrugs and runs his hand through his heavy hair. "Now where on earth are those shears? And that little silver hair decoration?" He rubs his eyes, readjusts his glasses, shuffles through a clipboard of papers, and draws the mino stand towards him again.

"Yes, fifteen at a time. Fifteen at a time."

Nakoshi is happy in his roomier workshop which is filled with the same orderly clutter as the old one. He has aged not a hair but continues to maintain calm control over the increasing number of kashira he must prepare. He notes only in passing that the troupe's recent policy of reviving old plays and seldom performed scenes requires research and additional work.

Repairer and Keeper of Heads

The troupe's resident repairer and keeper of puppet heads refinishes, restrings, and repairs heads, toggles, and limbs.

Working across from Nakoshi in the crowded head room is Koji Hishida, repairer of heads. "Some people call me the make-up man," Hishida says as he uses a white china mortar and pestle to mix the right shade of pink coating for refinishing the puppet head of a villain. "But it's more than getting the head the right color for the character." Hishida pauses to test the thickness of his mixture. "I've got to be sure that the complexion is the right shade of beige or pink, or a uniform white. But the details—the lines around the eyes, nose, and mouth and the bluish shading indicating shaved forelocks—vary according to the particular role in a play. Besides, the head has to be in proper working order."

Hishida picks up a white-haired male kashira by its headgrip and works the main toggle in front. "The most important toggle, the choi, controls the string that moves the head up and down. If the "nodding string" (*unazuki no ito*) isn't working properly, the doll is dead in every sense of the word, so I check it very carefully before turning the head over to a puppeteer. The leg operator and the head puppeteer himself will check it again every day before he performs, of course, because unless the choi is working properly, the kashira is worthless."

Holding the six-inch-long headgrip with his left hand so that the choi protrudes from between the middle and ring fingers, Hishida manages a smoothly

33. Whale baleen is the secret of the smooth nodding movements of puppet heads. Minosuke Oe examines large pieces before cutting off a small strip to use as a spring.

34. A left hand, a headgrip, and a right hand
(the shorter of the two) in Oe's workshop.

35. Oe checks a puppet head.

36. Heads in various stages of completion.

37. Nakoshi dresses the hair of a female puppet head as others wait their turn in the National Theatre in Tokyo.

38. A Bunshichi head for the role of Matsuomaru receives Nakoshi's
full attention in Osaka as he creates the "hundred-day's growth"
hairstyle. To his left is the wig-weaving (*mino*) stand.

39. Hishida refinishes a head in Osaka after carefully adjustin[g]
his gesso mix to suit the humidity and the temperature of the ai[r]

41. Mrs. Uehara works on a kimono sleeve; by her side is an appliance used to heat the small irons she uses as she sews puppet garments.

2. On the day before dress rehearsals t the National Theatre in Tokyo, tcho stitches an elaborate court costume into place to make his puppet.

0. Ishibashi repairs the ornate mbroidery of the outer robe orn by a courtesan.

43. Creating the proper line for his puppet claims Minosuke's full attention as he takes an extra tuck above a female puppet's obi.

44. Tamamatsu attaches a neckband to a puppet's understructure. A layer of gourd sponge is attached at the shoulders, a bamboo hoop at hip level. The *tsukiage bo* (support stick) that puppeteers cock on one hip to help them hold aloft large male puppets can be seen hanging below the waist hoop at the right.

menacing nod of the head. With his thumb, he works a small bamboo toggle at the back of the headgrip and the bushy eyebrows of the old man rise and fall realistically. Lowering another small toggle makes the eyes leer meanly to the left; another turns them far right. A ball of wadded paper on a string hanging down between the little toggles in the middle of the headgrip opens the mouth, and a particularly wicked expression is created by the contrast of the bright red tongue, the deep pink face, and the off-white hair.

Holding the head in the palm of his hand, Hishida carefully brushes on a fresh coat of pink. "Once that dries, I'll get back to it and give it light brown lines all around the eyes and across the bridge of the nose and around the nostrils. Darker lines to accentuate his mouth and to furrow his brow will make him look really evil."

Nakoshi laughs. "He looks mean already, even with all those fancy curls I spent so much time on, but wait till Hishida gets through with him!"

Hishida next picks up a Bunshichi head, the large white face topped by a huge tuft of black hair. "This one gets a bit of orange-brown shading around the eyes, the nose, and the corners of the mouth." He checks the movable brows. On the headgrip for this head, there is a fourth toggle which crosses the eyes and lifts the brows at the same time. "For the head inspection scene in *Sugawara Denju*—very important," says Hishida as the toggles click. He dips his brush into brown eye-liner paint and works on a tan Kintoki head.

"Now for some ladies," he says, laughing. "These sweet young things all have nice white complexions. This one had so many coatings of white built up on her that I had to soak them all off right down to the wood base and give her a completely new complexion. It took eleven layers of gesso and six sandpaperings between coats." Reaching for a large pottery grinding bowl with a ridged inner surface, he sprinkles in some caked white shell-lime powder. "Now for my secret recipe." He places a small saucepan solid with bone glue on an electric hot plate. "Doesn't smell too good." He stirs, then adds a bit of water and turns his attention back to the bowl.

"Have to get this gesso nice and fine," Hishida says, using a thick pestle the way a Japanese housewife crushes sesame seeds in an identical bowl. The only sound in the room is that of the wooden pestle grinding shell powder against the rough sides of the bowl.

Hishida stirs the pan of glue and pours a little into the white powder, adding a few drops of water. "Animal-bone glue and ground shells—but the proportions always vary a bit, depending on the weather." He stirs the mixture thoughtfully, now and then checking the thickness by letting some drip back into the bowl. Finally satisfied, he strains it into an enamel cup through several layers of gauze.

Picking up a female puppet head, he coats only the face with the thick white gesso, using a flat brush. "One coating should do for this girl," he says, laying the head down and turning to pick up another female kashira, this one a motherly type whose white coating has just dried. Suddenly he turns and starts frantically searching through piles of papers and heaps of brushes and jumbles of paint tins. After some rustling about, he extracts a small square of fine sandpaper from beneath his floor cushion and rubs it carefully across the cheeks and chin of the maternal head to add lustre.

"The young women get black eyebrows in most cases, but the brow shape depends on the head, the role, and the puppeteer's preference. Some like them thin, some like them very curved. Since the married women of Edo days shaved their eyebrows, most of them have just pale blue lines painted on, but the curve varies.

"Ouch!" Hishida cries out. "Well, at least I know she's got her mouth pin in properly." The *kuchibari* (literally, "mouth needle") is placed in the bottom lip of most middle-aged-woman heads and some young-woman heads also. When the puppeteer wants the woman to express grief, the kimono sleeve or hand towel can be caught on the pin, which is invisible to the audience, to make it look as if the woman was holding the material between teeth clenched in sorrow, frustration, or suppressed emotion. Sleeve-biting and towel-twisting are stylized gestures of female sorrow.

A puppeteer comes in with a pair of white legs and he and Hishida confer about repainting them *usu tamago* (literally, "pale egg;" beige) for a certain role. "That knee joint needs tightening," the doll manipulator says, "but the heel grips are just great on these. The curve of the metal fits my hands perfectly. I can do almost anything with these legs. If you could just get the knee fixed up in time for the tour . . . "

Another young puppeteer comes in, then another, both bearing legs they want refinished in white. Another brings a beige pair to be redone in pink. "It's like an epidemic—suddenly they all have leg problems. Incredible."

Hishida laughs, then turns up the radio by his side to listen to the horse races.

Just then an older puppeteer comes with a pair of white female hands. "These joints are just too loose, Hishida. What'll we do?" Hishida tries them out, nods, and agrees to repair the dainty hands immediately.

These are the most commonly used type of female hands, jointed at the wrists and also in the fingers at two places, and with pink lines painted in to accentuate each finger, each joint. The hands had been constructed by Oe like a sandwich—a layer of carved wood forms the back of the hand, and another, the palm and fingers. To allow flexibility of the joints, supple leather from an old shamisen is sandwiched between these layers. Many coats of gesso conceal the meticulous layering. There are many more complex hands, the ultimate being an intricate construction of wood, leather, and string, with every finger fully articulated. These *tako tsukami* ("octopus grip") hands are used by Matsuomaru, for instance, in *Sugawara Denju* and are remarkably expressive when used by a skilled puppeteer. A hand's action is controlled by a toggle connected at midarm to silk shamisen cords running from the hand through the carved wooden arm. Right-hand movement is controlled by the head puppeteer who uses the toggle as a lever; the left-arm toggle is worked by the left-arm manipulator whose right arm operates the sashigane, a wooden armature, which is attached to the puppet's left arm. The puppeteer moves the toggle within the armature by pulling or letting loose a band of twine, one loop controlled by the index finger, the other by the middle finger. The internal stringing of the cloth-jointed wooden legs and arms is done by Minosuke Oe at the time the limbs are originally carved but it is Hishida who keeps the strings in good working order.

Hishida finds a roll of used hides which once covered shamisen sound boxes, and chooses a piece of appropriate thickness. "This is just right for female hands, but we use a thicker leather for the big, fully-articulated hands of male dolls."

"Once you start appearing in good roles," a puppeteer in his early forties says, "you have to start accumulating your own sets of arms. The main puppeteer has to have puppet arms with hands appropriate for the role and for his techniques. All Bunraku arms and legs are individually owned by puppeteers. On tour, we pack them ourselves and carry them with us because they are as precious as our own limbs. Also, very expensive."

A youthful leg operator appears with a pair of puppet arms tied together and slung over his right arm and wearing a set of legs tossed over one shoulder.

"Tamao *shisho* (master) would like these recoated for the tour, please," this apprentice of puppeteer Tamao says politely. The large tako tsukami hands click as the thumbs and four fingers, each separately jointed in two places, dangle from the thick, jointed wrists. The lower arms are also carved wood finished in gesso, but the upper arms are of shaped and stuffed cotton cloth.

The young puppeteer spiritedly tries one arm, then the other, stepping in careful, long strides. He removes the set from his shoulders and reties them neatly with the lengths of twine that are attached to the tips of the padded upper arms. He hooks the set over a nail above Hishida's head. The hands sway; the puppeteer pats them still and leaves with a last quick glance over his shoulder.

"I've been repairing arms, legs, hands, heads, necks, headgrips and heel grips for twenty years," Hishida says, wiping perspiration off his forehead with his sleeve. "My father knew one of the set guys here and dragged me in to apprentice to the kashira repairer. Never thought I'd spend my life painting and stringing up parts. Nowadays I also do quite a bit of carving of heads. People say that's difficult, but at least it doesn't depend quite as much on the weather, the way this gesso mixing does."

Hishida puts away the shamisen skins, his mortar and pestle, the gesso, and his flat brushes. In a small dish, he mixes a brilliant red pigment and then dampens a thin, pointed brush. "A bit of lipstick for the ladies, and then for some head repairs."

Hishida has his familiar jumble of equipment in the new Osaka theatre. In addition to refinishing, he spends more time carving heads and limbs these days as Minosuke Oe delegates an increasing share of this to him. Hishida's cheerfulness as he works is as undiminished as that of Nakoshi with whom he shares a lively workshop.

Costumes

All costumes for Bunraku puppets are sewn by hand in the Osaka workroom to fit specific dolls and roles.

"In Bunraku, the puppet is the costume, the costume is the character," says Osamu Ishibashi as he sits on the tatami, folding the various parts of the costume that puppeteer Tamao will use to create Matsuomaru for the leading role in *Sugawara Denju*.

"The minute a puppet appears on stage, the audience knows the social status of the character and his general nature, as well as the type of play to be performed. The costumes show immediately whether the play is a historical drama or a domestic tragedy, a winter's tale or a summer episode. The clothes say right away that the character is a shogun or a shopkeeper, a farmer or a nobleman in disguise, a princess or a courtesan, good or evil."

Ishibashi presides over a storeroom stacked to the ceiling with silk kimonos, cotton jackets, embroidered velvet overgarments, and brocade obis. Collars, cords, aprons, work shirts, silk sashes, and princely brocades fill the drawers and cupboards. In his workroom and on his shelves, there is never a pile awry or an article out of place. Entire outfits are bundled together neatly with narrow lengths of silk carefully labeled by role and puppeteer; piles of folded robes are lined up precisely by type on open shelving to await Ishibashi's meticulous inspection before being returned to storage; a parcel of pleated silk hakama sits stiffly in a corner in need of mending; rolls of colored silk fabrics pave a cupboard with rainbows. In the holding room next door, fifty puppets swing from ropes, fully attired but lifeless without the heads and arms, which the puppeteers attach before going on stage.

"A puppet, after all, is simply a costume with a head attached. The costume plus limbs is the doll, and the costume in the hands of the puppeteer becomes the actor. Costumes are more than mere clothing or adornment in Bunraku. In creating and putting together costumes, I must keep in mind not only the play and the nature of the different characters in it, but also the manner in which the puppeteer creates a doll by putting together the costume I provide for him and by manipulating the puppet in his own individual style on stage."

Ishibashi is a calm man in his early forties who moves with quiet precision. His manner is matter-of-fact, but the way he handles the garments makes it clear that he enjoys his orderly world of fine fabrics. He is cheerfully at ease as he irons a thick, male costume.

"There are lots of conventions and precedents for Bunraku costumes, the most important one being that they are nearly all Edo-period garments. Also, certain patterns or colors have traditionally been used for specific roles in certain plays. That means that when I design a new costume for the role, I stay within these limitations. Naturally, other restrictions arise from the size of the doll and, particularly, its head type. I have to keep in mind the type of scenery and the lighting, traditional meanings of patterns and colors, established color harmony, and the aesthetic considerations involved in setting many puppets on stage at one time. But even more important than all these points is the basic fact that a costume must reveal the character of the person wearing it."

Ishibashi pulls out a long silk sash that is used tied below the obi on a young woman. "Now this shade of pink is all right for sweet Osono, the famous faithful "virgin wife" of *Hadesugata Onna Maiginu* (The Courtesan's Colorful Dance Robe) whose husband forsakes her for a courtesan, but the color is wrong for a courtesan. A more seductive pink has to be found. And this lovely soft gray-blue satin is perfect for a lord's wife. It has dignified elegance. A brighter hue would give the wrong impression of her character. For country people, bright stripes are out. They wear subdued hues so that yellow stripes must be dyed again to become ochre. And black—now that's very difficult. To be rich and elegant enough for Matsuomaru, for instance, the silk must be dyed red first to give the black depth. Otherwise, it's dingy, not suitable for a man of his noble character and high station."

Within the framework of aesthetics and tradition, it is up to Ishibashi to create costumes both for a new play and for old plays for which records no longer exist. "For revivals of a play or certain scenes not done for a century or more, I must decide on fabric, color, and pattern; have the material woven, dyed, and embroidered in Kyoto; and then work out the cut and accessories. This usually means discussions with the puppeteers also. I have detailed notes on all costumes I've dealt with in my six years here and from my twenty years working on Shochiku productions of Kabuki and dance."

From her low worktable in the corner of the room, Mrs. Uehara speaks without looking up from her sewing. "Those puppets move around so, more than humans, I'd say. I have to use really sturdy cotton so that the kimonos will hang properly on the framework. Even the silk robes need padding. You don't do all that for human actors, but the puppets need that to make them elegant. All that moving around is hard on the costumes. That's why I'm very busy every minute and never get caught up."

Mrs Uehara wears a friendly pout. Her smooth, fine skin is accentuated by the brownish hues of her curled hair. Her plump face is youthful and uncreased for all her sixty-two years, her eyes bright, and her hands strong but graceful.

"The puppets' kimonos are only one-half or two-thirds life size, but there's more work to one than for a real person. There are special little differences in the sleeves and the skirt, and there's the horizontal slit at the back, about six inches long, for the men to reach into to grasp the doll's headgrip."

Mrs. Uehara smooths out a white silk garment with delicate movements, measuring with a bamboo ruler that has turned amber from thirty year's use.

"The toughest material to sew is red silk. Natural safflower-plant dye, real *beni,* produces a wonderful crimson, really beautiful," she says, stroking the crimson lining of a collar on the shelf, "but I need good strong fingers to shove a needle through beni-dyed silk. The thimble helps. I make my own ring thimbles for the middle knuckle of my middle finger out of leather scraps from a man who makes baseball mitts. They're just right, soft but tough.

"And the needles—now they are a terrible problem. The only ones that are any good are the handmade needles, and just one type. But they don't sell them here in Osaka any more. It'll be a pretty pass for Bunraku when there are no decent needles for making costumes," she says with disgust.

She threads a short needle in a flash and, with visible effort, pushes it through the padded hem of the red silk kimono held taut by its anchor to the pincushion on one side and her hand on the other. "Really pretty, these costumes," she says with a hint of a smile before she becomes serious again. "Since this is my job, it's not important whether I like it or not, but I must admit I think this one is a particularly elegant robe."

Ishibashi sits tailor-fashion, running an iron over the white silk garments Matsuomaru and Chiyo will wear in their dance of lamentation in *Sugawara Denju*.

"Any silk garment is a living thing. Silk thread is spun by living silkworms and this gives the cloth woven from their thread a special vibrant quality. Silk has a special warmth and it's always changing. Silk garments really should be treated like human beings, you know—they only have one life on earth, like us. When a silk costume has endured a span of forty or fifty years, it comes to the end of its life. While it is new or still in good shape, however, a silk garment has remarkable qualities. It doesn't show its age and it springs back to life even after having become creased or wrinkled. Hanging it up or steaming it a little will restore it to its former beauty. Silk needs care just as human bodies do. But I assure you, silk is much nicer to work with than those dead materials like rayon, polyester, or even cotton."

"I do hate to see those lovely white silks get dirty," Mrs. Uehara says with a small sigh. "When the puppeteers finish with the dolls, they rip out all the stitching and pull the costumes off the frames. When the robes and sashes and other accessories are returned to us, we never know what state they will be in."

"Well, at least there's no make-up on them," Ishibashi says seriously. "This is funny work," he muses, "lonely work. We're hidden up here in the shadows, and there's never any applause and not even the puppeteers say much of anything unless something is wrong. But there is a satisfaction that comes when I peek at a scene or two and notice that things look right."

Mrs. Uehara uses an iron half the size of her palm on a kimono sleeve she has just cut out. "I like the quiet here," she says. "Why, when everyone is off in Tokyo or on tour, I'm all alone up here sewing. The only sound is the creaking of the pincushion stand or the squeaking of the needle. But I'll retire in three years. The trouble is they haven't gotten anyone to take my place. No successor, no needles—whatever is going to happen?"

"That is our biggest worry," Ishibashi agrees. "I just don't think people realize how complicated it is to get the costumes made and laid out so that every puppeteer has his proper bundle for every scene, every role, every play, every run."

Ishibashi climbs down into the adjoining storeroom, where he opens a drawer stuffed full of white silk neckbands. "One for Tamao—I know the length and width and softness he likes—and quite different ones for Minosuke and Bunjaku."

Ishibashi and Mrs. Uehara enjoy the spaciousness of their new quarters in the National Bunraku Theatre in Osaka. All the costume parts, on shelves and in drawers, and dozens of dressed puppet frames, hanging from rods, are now in one large room. Mrs. Uehara works at her old low table but Ishibashi has moved from the tatami to a desk for both paperwork and stitching and ironing. Every drawer and shelf appears crammed full, just as in the previous smaller quarters. Ishibashi's shelves of meticulously lettered notebooks recording each garment, piece by piece, for every role in every play performed by the troupe are also packed full.

Mrs. Uehara stayed on past retirement age since she felt an obligation to get the troupe properly arrayed in various new costumes for the opening of the new theatre. She is happily using the last third of a supply of handmade needles which the author located and presented to her in 1978.

Creation of a Puppet

The basic framework of a doll is simple. A carved wooden head attached to a headgrip is thrust down through an opening cut out of a wooden shoulder board. A length of material hangs from the front and back of the shoulder board (*kata ita*) and to the cloth is attached the bamboo hoop that serves as the hips. The doll's costume is sewn on to cover the framework or trunk, known as the *do*, of wood, cloth, and bamboo. Arms and legs are then tied to the shoulder board with lengths of rope. A horizontal slit in the back of the costume allows the chief puppeteer to reach inside to grasp the headgrip.

"People seem to think that a puppeteer grabs a costumed puppet out of a storeroom and then marches out on stage to move it about," says Minosuke, fingering a shoulder board, a polished piece of wood about the size and shape of a Japanese woman's zori. "If a puppeteer can't make a good doll, he'll never be good himself, and if he doesn't make his puppet himself, he doesn't have a doll."

At forty-three, Minosuke has a boyish face with soft, round contours. His eyes are bright but wary. Not given to small talk, he is less jocular, more introspective than most of his colleagues; but once his hand grips the headgrip of a puppet on stage, his expressionless face radiates a startling intensity, an almost sensuous glow.

"It all starts with the shoulder board," Minosuke continues in his low voice. "I shape it about eight inches long, three inches wide, and anywhere from about a quarter to an inch thick. I bevel and smooth the rounded shoulder ends of the board and the standard keyhole center opening for the headgrip.

"People cannot believe that the puppet's body is so simply constructed; they think we must add hidden mechanisms under the costume. Heavy cloth or paper stitched to the front and back of the shoulder board hangs down like an uninflated life vest, and into a seam at waist level goes the circle of bamboo to serve as hips. No gimmicks—just our fingers working the headgrip."

Minosuke attaches a strip of loofah (*hechima,*) in a curve over the end of the shoulder board. "These sponge strips we stitch on in overlapping layers to create the form of the shoulders. A young courtesan needs nicely rounded, fleshy shoulders; an old lady, narrow bent ones with less sponge. A warrior's shoulders will be high and wide, an old man's, sloping and low. Puppeteers make their own puppet frames, from carving the board to sewing on the sponge, in order to have many frames prepared for a variety of roles and to suit their individual tastes. Most of us have ten or twenty of them."

Minosuke unfastens a bundle of elaborate garments that make up one costume. He pulls out a fat cord of silk material and tests it for softness, flexibility, and width. "The costume director knows how I like this inner neckband, a bit soft but not too wide. If this is wrong, the whole doll is wrong."

Picking up a puppet's inner framework, Minosuke carefully finds the exact center of the stuffed collar (*naka eri*) and stitches it to the middle of the cloth hanging at the back of the shoulder board. "It's the first placement that makes all the difference in the doll," Minosuke says, draping the flexible sausage of white silk patterned in gold around the shoulder board. "The way the neckband curves around the neck and stands away from it has to be just right. The opening and the curve depend on how old the woman is, how seductive she's meant to be." Minosuke stitches on the inner neckband, which extends down to the bamboo hoop, in several places.

Next he attaches a flat, white silk neckband lined in crimson on top of the puffy one, delicately draping it so that several inches of crimson will peep out at bosom level when the doll is fully dressed. "This is the provocative way courtesans dressed," Minosuke remarks as he knots and snips. "It's not the bust line, it's the neckline, the back of the neck emphasized by the curve of the collar."

Picking up two kimonos layered one inside the other—a long scarlet kimono with an embroidered neckband over an under kimono of printed silk—he proceeds to attach them to the puppet's trunk so that the edge of each of the four neckbands shows. Minosuke props the kimono-covered framework on a bamboo stand before him, then drapes the gowns, checking them from the front, the sides, and the back. He stitches, snips, knots, smooths the hems, adjusts the crossover. Throwing the long sleeves of the kimonos up onto the shoulders, Minosuke tucks the garments to create a flat bust line.

"This is one of the most difficult parts of the kimono line because it's vital to the characterization. Courtesans flatten their bosoms so there must be only the trace of a curve here. A low-class prostitute would accentuate her breasts. For a nice young city girl, there's no curve either, but for one who's married and had a child or two, it's all right to stitch the kimono to indicate that her breasts are larger, softer, and not bound. An older country woman would be dressed to give a careless, even sagging bust line; a court lady would be neat and erect. These stitches establish the attractiveness of the female character, her sensuousness, her age, her social position and marital status, so they must be done with great care."

Minosuke continues molding the courtesan out of crepe and brocade, stitches and concealed knots. He wraps a brocade obi, stiffened with cardboard, around the waist and attaches it, then sews the obi's huge hanging bow to the front. "Harder work physically," he says, prodding the needle slowly through the heavy band, "but the skill lies in the first collar and the bosom line."

Minosuke turns the doll and peers critically at it, tilting his head and squinting at it from several angles. "With the big headdress she'll have, this should be right. Sometimes I get the whole doll made and then become dissatisfied when I place the head in the trunk. It usually means that the first neckband is not on right, so I rip it all apart and start all over again. Depends on how I'm feeling. Some days, the pieces go on well; other times, no amount of stitching and adjustment will produce what I want. Depends on my mood."

Minosuke calls his two young assistants, who have been making their own small dolls representing children, to finish the costuming of the courtesan. They insert a square of red silk to fill the space where the kimono falls open at the hem, and they stitch and make tucks in the inside hems to provide tufts of material for the leg operator to pinch hold of when he manipulates the kimono skirt on stage to give the illusion of walking, running, or sitting.

Minosuke returns to unpack his own set of wooden arms and he gropes under the heavy costume to tie them firmly to the shoulder board.

"A puppeteer knows from the back how the dolls look from the front. I've been behind puppets ever since I was seven, when I began training with my father and was apprenticed to Bungoro. We learn to make a doll by observing and by having the master find fault with what we've done. Bungoro told me what was wrong, so I learned what was right."

Minosuke worked with Bungoro for eight years, and from 1948 he was the leading apprentice of Monjuro II until the latter died in 1970 at the age of seventy. Like his masters, Minosuke is known for the delicacy and elegant eroticism he brings to female roles, especially those requiring dancing and a variety of poses.

"I work out in my mind how the role should be done before I pick out the proper puppet frame and make the doll. The personality, the attractiveness must be thought out and balanced carefully in the doll so that the physical appearance of the puppet matches the characterization I emphasize with movement on stage.

"People say we dress a puppet, put a costume on a doll. That's incorrect. A puppeteer *creates* a doll, and this is one of the joys of Bunraku, one of the challenging pleasures of the life of a head puppeteer. But if the mood is wrong—well, you start all over again." Minosuke gives a cautious laugh. "At the neckband."

A young puppeteer brings Minosuke the courtesan head to be used for the role. The face is white, fleshy, voluptuous, the coiffure ornate. Minosuke checks the main toggle. There are no small toggles on this headgrip since eyes and mouth are immobile. Minosuke inserts the headgrip in the dressed puppet body and adjusts the angle of the courtesan's head.

Down the hall, Tamao starts to work constructing a male doll in another dressing room. He turns a padded neckband over and over in his hands, then positions it on the large puppet frame which hangs on a low bamboo stand in front of him, and plunges in a needle. "It's the first stitch that counts," Tamao says with a grin. He is soon lost in concentration on the second neckband. Undergarments and robes are added quickly in layers and firmly fastened. "The stitching for male dolls must be particularly strong since they move about so much. It takes a man's strong hands to do this," Tamao says, "but we must be careful not to pierce our fingers. Our fingers are our life."

In still another dressing room, Sakujuro is working on the neckband for a huge warrior, the type of blustering role for which he is best known. "If that first stitch is right, the rest goes well—unless you're just not with it that day. That happens some days."

Tamako, who shares the dressing room, mumbles agreement as he bends over a puppet frame resting on his lap, a threaded needle clenched between his teeth. "Once you've gotten that inner neckband on right, the battle is half won. And anyone who can't make a doll up right is no puppeteer. Sloppy doll, sloppy operator. The kimono tucked up a wee bit in front adds a bit of class to a male doll, makes him look smart. It's these little touches we keep in mind."

Several hours later, every dressing room is adorned with puppets. Gradually the junior puppeteers move the costumed puppet bodies out onto the shelf in the hallway.

The dressing rooms in the new Osaka theatre and in Tokyo are roomy enough to accommodate the dressed puppets, although tsume are still relegated to the hallway. Puppeteers devote the day before the standard two days of stage rehearsal to creating their puppets, known as *ningyo tsukuri* (literally, "puppet creation") or *mae goshirae* (literally, "making ahead"). For the Tokyo run and tours, they usually assemble and stitch costume parts onto the puppet frames in Osaka. These are packed and shipped and the puppeteers then finish or adjust them, often extensively, in Tokyo or on the road. The head puppeteer ties the arms onto the shoulder board; the leg operator attaches the legs and sews on the leggings or tabi and obtains the footgear and headgear from the prop man.

Props

The props (*kodogu*) of Bunraku are varied and many. The categories include hand props, headgear and footgear, stage props, animals, and severed heads and limbs. Props are kept on stage only for the short periods of actual stage business, after which they are whisked off stage by apprentice puppeteers.

In a long wooden shack deposited as an afterthought on the roof of the Asahi Theatre, a gray-haired man searches one shelf and then another, and extracts a pair of swords, four pairs of straw sandals, gold coins, and a round box with a crude model of a child's head.

"I have everything we need for Bunraku plays up here in this crowded store-room," Eijiro Yonetani says. "It's just a matter of finding it. The two men who help me with props just haven't figured out my system yet. Sandals, tabi, clogs, any sort of footgear and headgear are my responsibility, not the costumer's. All the hand props, like towels, fans, and pipes, as well as movable stage props, like armor boxes and lanterns—these are all up to me to gather and distribute. Passing them out isn't the problem. The headaches come in making sure I get everything back."

Yonetani consults his notebook and checks off items needed for the next tour, as an assistant groups them together on a shelf outdoors. "I've memorized lots of prop lists but use my notebooks to double-check. Two crystal Buddhist rosaries, a writing box with a child's shroud inside, the round head box—make sure it's the child's head, not one of the adult heads we have up here—and the writing brushes and paper for all the children in the school scene. And the palanquin," Yonetani continues as the two men start to pack the props for *Sugawara Denju* in a burlap case.

"One of the hardest things to keep track of in *Katsuragawa* is that gray stone. Well, it looks like a stone but it's just a stuffed flannel bag. The lovers Ohan and Choemon pick it up one after another and pretend to place it in their sleeves, as if they were loading their kimonos with heavy stones in order to drown faster when they commit suicide in the Katsura River. It's an important prop in getting across the whole idea of their determination to die, but it's up to the left-arm operators to keep receiving and handing over the stone to the head puppeteers and then the leg operator is meant to return the stone to me."

Smoking sets, floor cushions, towels, lanterns, brooms, and dusters crowd the shelves. A papier-mâché male head, its stump of a neck painted red, lies casually in a box next to a bloodied arm and two legs. "The mobile arms and legs belong to the puppeteers, but when a limb is to be cut off on stage, it's up to me to provide a substitute separate arm, leg, or head that looks properly gory and that suits the character who has lost it."

Yonetani goes to the end of the closet to check on a horse. "I keep all the animals together. Horses have to be kept in good repair, both for the men who wear them over their heads and the puppets who mount them. Various types of foxes are very important in Bunraku plays, but they really are a problem. Some of my foxes are getting a bit scruffy looking, but it costs a fortune to get a new one made—have it cut out of flannel, stuffed, whiskered and yes, spotted properly—so I just struggle along with the ones I have, giving them a good cleaning now and then. The wild boar is only visible for a few seconds as a puppeteer dashes across stage with him in *Kanadehon Chushingura* but he's vital to the plot. I have tigers, deer, eagles, dogs, and water birds too.

"And in the food department, pickled plums, broiled fish, the octopus for the teahouse scene in *Chushingura,* rice (just cotton wool), and poisoned cakes, as well as teapots, cups, sakè bottles, chopping knives, and dishes. The only fresh food I need is a big daikon, the white radish Omitsu slices in a kitchen scene— I have to run out and buy a fresh one every few days. Flowers? I have all varieties, including several colors of chrysanthemums that turn limp when poisoned sakè is poured over them. Poison is used a lot in Bunraku."

Downstairs during a play, Yonetani stands guard at the three black shelves that line the corridor leading from the wings to the puppeteers' dressing rooms.

He prods a left-arm operator to return a sword, one leg manipulator to surrender a bunch of coins, another, a paper umbrella. The props are a startling mixture of life-size articles originally made for human use (tobacco pouches, for instance) and miniature pieces scaled slightly too large for the puppets but easily identifiable by the audience.

It is Yonetani who gathers together all the props necessary for any one program. The leg manipulator obtains the prop from Yonetani just before the appropriate scene and sees to it that it is in the hands of a hidden assistant, the *kaishaku,* usually a very junior puppeteer, on stage. This kaishaku, crouched low behind the stage partition, hands the item up to the left-arm operator in time for use by the puppet. Once the prop is seen and understood by the audience, the left-arm operator hands it back down to the hidden assistant who removes it. This continual process of supplying the correct prop at the right time and then whisking it away after use is an undercurrent of all action on stage.

Another unseen labor of the prop master is supplying tall black prop tables on which, in long scenes, puppets in sitting positions rest their legs or heavy props such as large swords or a head-inspection box. The flimsy wooden stands, painted black, are light and narrow enough to fit in almost anywhere. These stands, or *rendai,* are just barely lower than the top of the stage partitions that hide the puppeteers from hip-level down. They are thus invisible beyond these partitions and the audience is not conscious of their use. The use of these stands did not become prevalent until some forty years ago: until then, junior puppeteers were responsible for holding the props up in their hands at the proper level or propping up the legs of a large doll in heavy armor enough to make long scenes less excruciating for chief puppeteers standing motionless. The stands are carried out of the way by the youngest puppeteers or the prop man the minute they are no longer needed.

"It's the props that give the young puppeteers their start on stage. The young fellow squats backstage holding a tray of food or a gory model of a head. He learns when and where to hand the tray to the left-arm operator for the puppet's stage business, and he learns to whisk the chopped-off head up onto a prop stand to replace the puppet's real head just after the character is decapitated by the enemy. Good timing is essential and of course that's how the young puppeteers learn the plays. I was a puppeteer myself for years, until I lost a leg during the war, so I know the importance of having the prop in exactly the right place at the right time."

A young puppeteer in black runs by to consult the cue book hanging near puppeteer Tamao's door. "In the next part he's got to be in charge of several props by the stage-center door," says Yonetani. "It's never boring. Besides, if you don't learn the importance of a prop when you start out in Bunraku, you might as well quit right then and there. You have to pay attention every minute because a puppet can't just lean down and pick up a dropped dagger or a forgotten teacup. Bunraku is made up of small details, one added to another, then another. Handling a sword, holding up a fox, lighting a courtesan's pipe, sliding in a hidden black table on which to place a smoking set so that the audience thinks the box rests on the tatami—are all part of Bunraku."

The young puppeteer walks back to the wings. Yonetani is engrossed in counting stage coins.

In the new National Bunraku Theatre in Osaka, props are kept in a large room, lined with shelves from top to bottom, on the third floor and in a basement storeroom. Both Yonetani and his assistant have retired. Tokiyo Wada is now in charge of props. Puppeteer Tamanosuke works with him, appearing only occasionally on stage, because his familiarity with Bunraku props and puppeteers' needs in that area make him an essential member of the prop team. Toshimichi Kawashima of the Fujinami Kodoguya, the family firm that for centuries has been the official supplier of props to Kabuki and Bunraku, often assists Wada (as a representative of Fujinami, since he is not a member of the Bunraku troupe).

The third-floor room is neatly organized by Wada who has fifty or so swords neatly displayed on horizontal racks, staves, halberds, and spears in vertical ones, and shelves with boxes, carefully labeled, holding the coins, cushions, pipes, brushes, letters, lanterns, smoking and drinking sets, and other props that are vital in Bunraku plays. Wada is compiling his own prop notebooks since his predecessors took their precious documents with them. Animals, futons, palanquins, ox-drawn carts, and other bulky items are stored in the basement. A new fox made its debut in the theatre's opening performance and a particularly lifelike tiger delighted the July 1984 audience.

The active prop room is in the wings, stage-left, a switch from the stage-right position of the Asahi-za that takes getting used to. Since the majority of puppets make stage-right entrances, auxiliary shelves have been placed there. Tamanosuke and

Wada are kept busy arranging props near both stage-right (*shimote*) and stage-left (*kamite*) entrances. Both confess to feeling nervous that an important pipe or floor cushion will get misplaced now that puppeteers know there are two locations for picking up props. "They're supposed to return them to us at kamite but we have a devil of a time keeping track of things," Wada says. Tamanosuke says he spends the entire play scurrying from one side to the other.

Ohayo Gozaimasu!

The heavy glass doors of the Asahi-za's small stage entrance on Sakai Suji squeak open to a chorus of morning greetings. *"Ohayo gozaimasu!"* (good morning!) calls out a young tayu. He slips out of his shoes, places them in the compartment marked with his name, and scurries down the hall to his dressing room. "Ohayo gozaimasu!" shouts the old man who checks the comings and goings from his desk by the stage door, peering over his glasses to make sure the youngster has turned over the wooden plaque marked with his name on the attendance board. "Ohayo gozaimasu!" says the first-floor tea lady cheerfully, and "Ohayo gozaimasu!" echoes a young puppeteer as he dashes back out the door on his first errand for his master.

Two young shamisen players enter chatting, then they too sing out together, "Ohayo gozaimasu! Ohayo gozaimasu!"

Through the stage doors come young musicians, narrators, and puppeteers, all intent on being in their dressing rooms before their elders. The costume seamstress comes in at her accustomed hour, and her measured progress up to the fourth floor can be traced by the sound of her matter-of-fact voice calling out good morning.

The middle-ranking puppeteers start to swagger in, laughing and joking between loud greetings. A younger puppeteer slips through a knot of older ones, bowing and calling out a strong "Ohayo gozaimasu!" to each man before he runs down the hall and takes the stairs two at a time to the puppeteers' floor. The older men's vigorous footsteps sound evenly along the first-floor corridor already filled with the first begrudging notes of a shamisen being tuned and with a clearing of throats and a few hoarse syllables by several young tayu.

Up on their own floor, the puppeteers make their rounds of morning greetings, and the whole building seems to throb with energy. Men dart in and out of dressing rooms unbuttoning their smart sport shirts, tying narrow obi around their cotton kimonos, adjusting their black tights, fashioning the large bows that close their black performance gowns. Puppeteers take attendance of puppets propped up on bamboo stands in their rooms and outside in the corridor.

The first greeting of the day in Bunraku is always "Ohayo gozaimasu!" whether it is nine in the morning or even three in the afternoon when a senior musician comes to prepare for his late afternoon performance. Junior members of the troupe come to their feet to bow and voice their greetings as a senior tayu makes his solemn progress down the hall at four o'clock for his apprentice's performances. He will dress later for his own appearance on stage at seven in the evening.

In the corridors, on the street at lunch time, or in the wings during the evening performance, when a member of Bunraku first glimpses a colleague, he calls out "Ohayo gozaimasu!" Later meetings are acknowledged with a quick nod of the head or a smile, or are completely, mutually, and politely ignored by both in the knowledge that etiquette had been properly followed earlier. "If we happen to meet on the last train home at night, passengers give us odd looks when we call out a morning greeting," says a puppeteer, "but even offstage, only 'Ohayo gozaimasu' is correct for the first encounter of the day."

In a crowded dressing room, a middle-aged puppeteer chats as he checks the toggles and rods on the arms of two puppets he will be using, while an older colleague adjusts the length of the leg on his large doll. "That guy just doesn't greet people properly. There's no excuse for saying only 'Ohayo.' Where are his manners?" The puppeteer complains that this young man has also been addressing his seniors in familiar terms, as he would talk to a younger colleague, rather than using the usual forms, the honorific equivalent of 'Mr.' (Monju-san or Kanju-san, for instance) or the term 'older brother' (Monju *nii-san* or Kanju *nii-san*), a respectful designation used by members when addressing someone senior.

The culprit appears with a pair of puppet legs and a pair of arms clattering together as they swing from his arm. "And mind how you treat those limbs," the veteran puppeteer says gruffly. "They may need refinishing but they're valuable pieces of mine. Treat them with respect." The men work in silence interrupted only by the appearance of an occasional junior troupe member, who kneels and calls out his greeting at the threshold, as is customary until he reaches a certain level of seniority.

The code of etiquette, with its greetings and honorifics used before, during, and after performances, is one of the many conventions of Bunraku life that lubricate the wheels of communal living for this group of some eighty men who are committed to spending their lives performing together. A scolding in a dressing room, a muttered dissatisfaction over a role or a kashira assigned for use, a missed cue, a wrong note, an argument over a beer late the night before—all are set aside, swept permanently out of sight, as the members of the community greet each other on each new day of the Bunraku life they will share until the end.

"Kizaemon's wife was very strict about manners," says Kanju, a thirty-two-year-old puppeteer, as he stands in the wings bowing cheerfully to a senior narrator. "She was the wife of the great shamisen player who died recently at the age of eighty-five. She was a wonderful woman. My family was very poor, and she was the kind of lady who did nice things for everyone in the neighborhood.

"When I was only ten she took me to a Bunraku performance at a department store theatre and then asked me which I wanted to be: a puppeteer, a narrator, or a musician." Kanju laughs and shakes his head at the memory. "Since puppets are what attract people to Bunraku initially, I said I'd like to operate puppets. Well, a few days later, before I knew it, I had a place with Monjuro, the puppeteer.

"It was several years before I touched a puppet, but Kizaemon's wife made me come by every morning to open up the sliding shutters, to say good morning and to chat with her properly, and then to take her dog for a walk. After school, another conversation, another walk with the dog, and then off I'd go to Monjuro's house to sweep, scrub floors, and run errands. I used to go backstage with him to make tea, hand him towels, move his zori from one stage entrance to another, and to watch by the hour. I got teased because all I had to wear was my school uniform, but I kept watching.

"I trained under Monjuro for ten years, and thanks to his strictness, I learned a great deal. He was exacting but never mean. There's all sorts of discipline in Bunraku, and learning the manners and serving your elders are part of becoming a leg manipulator. Kizaemon's wife was always after me about etiquette, saying how important it is in Bunraku. I guess she scared it into me." He nods as if recalling her voice. "Manners are part of disciplined training, and that's what Bunraku is—discipline."

Looking around to make sure that none of his elders are about, a tayu in his early thirties seats himself tentatively on a bench in the wings to chat with a puppeteer his age. The young tayu has had only three years with the troupe since graduating from the formal Bunraku training program established in 1972 by the Bunraku Association and the National Theatre in Tokyo.

"Learning the proper greetings was very difficult at first," the bright-eyed tayu says. "There's 'I respectfully request your goodwill,' 'I am making a request for your kind assistance,' 'Thank you very much,' 'You have tired your-self greatly,' 'Thank you for your trouble,' and, for opening day of a run and the last day, 'Congratulations.' The trick is to know exactly when, to whom, and in what order to use them because it's all according to whether it's opening day, or the first greeting, or the end of a performance. Seniority is the most difficult thing to remember at first because it's not determined by age, but according to when the man joined the troupe. You have to learn to greet your elders in the proper order. It was terrifying at first trying to keep all those facts in my mind, but it's starting to come naturally now." The young man leaps to his feet and bows as a middle-aged musician walks calmly through the wings on his way to platform.

"I started out, after graduation from the two-year course, by going to my master's house every morning to clean the house, help with the cooking, and do errands. This discipline is good because it allows you to absorb the feelings and spirit of your teacher. I had several hours of practice with him and more chores, and when I got back to my own room there was no time for anything but a bit more studying. After two years of that, I was freed from most of the chores by a younger tayu, so now I go to my master's house every morning just for a lesson.

"My voice still doesn't do what I want it to do, and I seem to discover new difficulties of being a tayu every day, but I don't dream about ten or twenty years from now. I concentrate on doing the best I can right now. I don't think about being a good tayu but only about learning all I can and training every day so that someday my words will come out the way my teacher says they should."

Koshijidayu, a tayu who bears the distinction of being the oldest narrator in the troupe and the senior of its three "living national treasures" sits in his dressing room. He hums softly as he glances through his text and chats with the young apprentices.

"The young chaps nowadays have it so easy," he says with an air of detachment. His expression is one of continual but controlled surprise, and there is a reserve about him that is not unfriendly but nevertheless cool. "When I started my training as a small boy, it was ages before my teacher would even let me hear him. Oh, I went to his house every day, but all I did was open shutters, start the charcoal fires, make tea, scrub and sweep and clean. Then suddenly he had me listen to him. He gave me three chances to hear him do a fifteen minute portion of text, once a day for three days. Then he said, 'Do it!' He listened as I did it, striking the table before him with a wooden stick bound with old shamisen strings. He listened to me once, then two more times, correcting me and scolding me each time, and then that was the end of it. He never taught me that piece of narration again. It nearly drove me crazy, it was so nerve-wracking. I had to listen with every ounce of strength in my body and every scrap of concentration in my mind. But that severe training made me learn, and what I learned I have never forgotten. It was training in total absorption, which later helped me to store up in my brain all sorts of bits of phrasing by this tayu, the intonation of another, a rhythm here, a beat, a melody, an accent, or a modulation as I heard them from the lips of my predecessors. Now I am able to draw on this memory bank and to incorporate the strong points in my own performance." Koshijidayu gives a harsh laugh, rubbing the parchment-like skin of his high forehead with a large, square hand.

"It is important that we stay on the tracks of tradition without getting shunted off onto a siding, sent off into unknown territory, or being derailed. But if we notice no motion at all, if we just glide along, it would mean Bunraku had become boring, static. To keep Bunraku dynamic, it's essential to bring together the best of what is traditional but to discard the features that seem weak."

Koshijidayu's slim figure is erect as his hands tap out an irregular rhythm on his dressing table. "Severe training keeps you alert and able to absorb the best of what you hear. This business of tapes and being soft on apprentices— I don't think this is doing them any favors. Of course, I'm considered the

45. (*above left*) A falcon's talons are checked by one prop man as another holds a severed head.
46. (*above right*) A prop fox (left) rests on a pair of stage geta, while a female puppet in a "fox kimono" and with special paws for hands sits in a puppeteer's arms. Both appear in *Ashiya Doman Ouchi Kagami*.
47. (*below left*) Tsume ladies-in-waiting are assisted with their bird cages by assistants in the wings.
48. (*below right*) Butterflies await their cue, as a junior puppeteer prepares to wield the black stick to which they are attached.

49. Stagehands at work on the stage at the National Theatre in Tokyo during a rehearsal break. The geza is above the crested entrance curtain stage right; the yuka, stage left.

50. Tamao directs placement of the stone lantern used in the Ikudama scene of *Sonezaki Shinju*.

51. (*above*) Sakujuro (right) and Minotaro (left) watch a rehearsal, the front flaps o their hoods raised to show the metal armature each puppeteer devises to keep the cloth off his face.

52. (*below*) Tamao with Tokubei and Monju with the maid, assisted by junio puppeteers, adjust the position of the screen on the veranda for the elopement by night that marks the dramatic ending of the Temmaya scene of *Sonezaki Shinju*.

53. In an elaborate scene, puppeteers walk across the stage behind the boat (made from a flat) which, pushed by a puppeteer, glides on rollers across the stage as the boatman puppet rows realistically. Tamao (rear, in darkness) oversees the boatful of puppets and operators even at the final stages of rehearsal.

54. Nakoshi checks a tour roster as Hishida packs puppet heads for *Sugawara Denju* into padded bags—one decorated with a sketch of the head it protects.

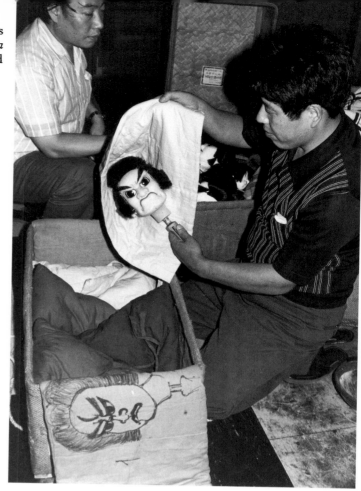

55. Kanjuro with Matsuomaru in the Terakoya scene of *Sugawara Denju*.

56. In the dressing room shared on tour by puppeteers, narrators, and shamisen players, puppeteer Tamame prepares for an appearance.

strictest teacher in the troupe—I'm really tough on them!" The young men laugh nervously as he glances at them. "But only with a strict training will they master the fundamentals of creating a voice and then using it properly."

The room is silent. Koshijidayu rises, and his apprentices jump to assist him in preparing to go on stage. He leaves accompanied by a silent cluster of men in cotton kimonos. Some fifteen minutes later, Komatsudayu, one of the group, returns.

"As long as the introductory narrative passage goes smoothly, all is well. Koshijidayu's voice is fine, but since his serious operation a few years ago he has had to take special care of his health. I will return to the wings to accompany him back here after he has completed his performance. That is a part of the etiquette."

Komatsudayu's wavy hair, combed back from a small widow's peak, accentuates his boyish face, his lively eyes, and his serious expression, which breaks occasionally into a slow, controlled smile. His speaking voice is low and gentle, just one tone above a whisper. On stage, his voice has clarity, fine timbre, and great flexibility. His bass is rich, his tenor virile, and his projection of feminine tones gentle, lacking the harshness of the falsetto used by some tayu.

"The greatest challenge for a tayu is to achieve a balance between realism and exaggeration in expression, between truth and beauty in narration. In domestic dramas, portraying the problems of ordinary people artistically is hard. In historical plays, the emotions of men and women of heroic proportions must be made credible. Throughout both, the tayu must maintain rhythm and clear enunciation.

"When you're young it's also hard to realize that simply changing your voice from high to low, or gentle to raucous will not get across characterization or the meaning of the lines. Unless you project the proper feeling, a change in voice will not convey a change in emotions.

"That's why dialogue is so difficult. Narrative passages are important, especially the beautiful lyric ones, but the recitative passages involving seven characters in lively conversation are a real challenge.

"I chose the way of Bunraku myself; to grow in skill, to achieve harmony within myself, I must be at peace with my decision. Emptying myself of my own emotions and creating a void to allow the play to speak for itself is my goal. When I am able to achieve selflessness, there is an indescribable joy at the end of the performance that comes from the unity achieved by puppeteers, tayu, musician, and audience, a special unity that lifts performers out of themselves.

"Only early hard training can bring rewards in Bunraku, and now that I have students to teach, it is my responsibility to impart what I have learned from tayu and shamisen players who have shared this tradition with me. I have much more training ahead, and many, many roles I hope to do. After all, I'm only forty-five."

More than half the members of the troupe today joined Bunraku at the age of fifteen or under, some as young as seven or eight. Immediately upon being apprenticed to a master, the lad is given a stage name by which he is known to all his colleagues. His personal name is seldom known to more than a handful of performers. As the young man develops skills, he progresses up the ladder by merit. Seniority is based on the number of years of membership, not age, but the pace at which men move to different levels of competence varies greatly. The age at which they are assigned to more important roles or portions of the text or music depends on demonstrated talent.

Family line means little in Bunraku, in contrast to Kabuki where family ties often allow less-talented members of important stage families to rise high despite artistic limitations. In any case, in the Bunraku troupe, there are fewer than a dozen men who are second-generation performers and only one, Midoridayu, who represents the third generation in his family to perform. Stage surnames for puppeteers are limited to Yoshida, Kiritake, and Toyomatsu; Toyotake and Takemoto for narrators; and Nozawa, Tsuruzawa, and Takezawa for shamisen players. All are names of historical significance. First names for performers usually incorporate a syllable of the master's stage name, and subsequent changes are chosen from the roster of past performers, with the most illustrious reserved for those with undeniable talent.

"My father was the first one in his family to enter Bunraku, but he achieved the illustrious name of Tamazo IV," says Tamamatsu. "As a kid, I hadn't planned to follow in his footsteps. I started off as a child actor in popular comedies with my uncle in Osaka and Tokyo, but two years was enough. I joined Bunraku as an apprentice of Tamaichi II when I was thirteen and, after his death, became an apprentice to Monjuro II in 1949. In thirty years, I've been known as Tamaichiro, Mon'ya, and now Tamamatsu, and who is to know whether I will ever become Tamazo V?"

Tamamatsu is a short, wiry man of forty-four whose happy-go-lucky nature and ready laugh make him a lively member of the troupe. Since he is one of the shortest performers in Bunraku, just over five feet, he is often teased about the height of his stage clogs.

"Since I'm short, I've had to devise special ways to use my body and my small hands to manipulate the puppets. But then, everyone has to work out his own style once he has learned the fundamentals.

"Our generation learned well," Tamamatsu says, flicking his small fingers from one toggle to another as he checks a headgrip.

"We were scolded or hit if we did something wrong—no hard feelings, we were just wrong—so we learned to be right. I've had ten years with the legs, ten with the left arm, and ten as chief puppeteer.

"All the years of training blend together when three puppeteers begin to move a single doll at dress rehearsal. Having observed the part when young, having mastered the manipulative movements, and having studied the script, each one knows what is expected of him. That's why those years with the legs count so much. And if the legs aren't right, that puppet dies no matter what the head puppeteer does. It can drive you crazy if you're on stage as head puppeteer—you can tell right away when the legs go wrong, and there's nothing you can do then except maybe mutter directions to the inexperienced leg manipulator.

"All three puppeteers must focus on the back of the doll's head. If that is not the focal point, and if they do not extend their senses to the doll's every movement, everything just falls apart. For the doll to be alive, all three must *be* together—must share intuition and must feel that they are inseparable. One plus one plus one equals more than three in Bunraku, but three minus one equals zero.

"Bunraku is not something you just drop into for a few years. It's for life, and you have a goal to work for from the start," Tamamatsu says seriously as he pulls apart the leggings on a puppet and then proceeds to restitch them. "That early training not only teaches us doll operation but also how to get along with each other. You have to be able to operate a doll with any other puppeteer. You can't bear grudges or decide you can't work with someone in

Bunraku. I'll kid around with a puppeteer my age and tell him that he came in too quickly or that his movements are too broad, but in a friendly way because I want him to do it to me also—to my face, not behind my back. We're all in this together. The whole point of Bunraku is to give a good performance, not to show off individually.

"My generation of puppeteers—we all were in training together and we lived, breathed, ate, and even drank Bunraku. We talked about it constantly, and as we rode the streetcars at night, the tayu's words would go through our minds and we'd think of hand and finger movements.

"The young chaps today divide their Bunraku time from their leisure time. They even play cards backstage. We watched everything that went on. It comes in handy later to remember how a pose was achieved, an eye movement timed, or a costume moved. Oh sure, we had our fun and our drinking and our playing around, but even when we aren't working, we're always thinking about it. Bunraku is always there, just below the surface. After all, our life is Bunraku. We *are* Bunraku."

Downstairs, a senior tayu says, "We leave our personal identities behind to join this group dedicated to performance. Competitive spirit keeps us trying harder. We notice sometimes that when an old performer dies, the man considered his chief rival loses some spirit. This is because some of the desire to compete is gone. It's good to keep alive that spark caused by the friction of rival talents. In Bunraku we can only function as a group, but competition serves to goad us on towards the common goal."

Another narrator, Mojitayu, says: "There is no such thing as being satisfied with your performance when you are a tayu. You may think to yourself, 'Well, the old woman's part was all right, and the young man, but the old man just didn't come off.' After all, we don't learn just one role—we shift back and forth between many, so it's almost impossible to be satisfied. Besides, I'm only fifty-three, and in Bunraku one is not considered a true performer until one reaches fifty, and not an artist at all until one reaches sixty. We say it takes three years to learn to laugh, eight years to learn to cry. Well, that's only the beginning. That may be enough to learn how to do it, but not to do it well."

In Kanjuro's dressing room, Tamao and Kanjuro are engrossed in casting a play. They lean over a small folding table, the size of an airline food tray, as Kanjuro reaches for a battered tin box that once held twenty round hard candies. He unsnaps the container and thirty-one tiny wooden wafers tumble out, each one inscribed with the name of a puppeteer, in red ink on one side, black on the other. As if setting up a chess game, the two men slide the tablets about, finally agreeing on an arrangement. Groupings of three wafers indicate the combination of puppeteers who will operate each puppet, names in red for the chief puppeteer, the wafer inscribed in black to its right and above for the left-arm manipulator, to its left and below for the leg operator. Single wafers represent one-man dolls; placed in another position, a single name indicates that the man will serve as hidden stage assistant. The arrangement of wafers shifts as the men go through each scene. A left-arm manipulator appears in a later portion of a scene as a chief puppeteer; a leg operator will serve as a hidden prop handler as needed. Several junior puppeteers are designated to take turns making the familiar "Tozai" announcements at the beginning of scenes or portions thereof, depending on the timing of their stage appearances as puppet manipulators. Even senior head puppeteers often appear as left-arm operators to work with younger head puppeteers. All the details of the shifting functions of the puppeteers as doll handlers and stage assistants are then written out in special calligraphy by Kanjuro in the *kowaricho*, or role-assignment book. Once this book is in order, Bunjaku is able to choose the puppet heads for the assigned roles. Assigning roles, functions, and puppet heads for any one run usually takes place in the last days of the preceding run.

The long cue book is draped over the stage-front partition during dress rehearsals but hangs outside Kanjuro's or Tamao's room during the run. On the day devoted to making the puppets and arranging props (the day immediately before the standard two days of dress rehearsals for Tokyo and Osaka runs), the old-fashioned traditional Japanese-style note book lies on the tatami in Kanjuro's dressing room where it is constantly consulted by young puppeteers who are responsible for working out on their own exactly where to position themselves during the play. In one scene, the young chap may be the one to bring props on stage to hand over to a certain puppet's leg operator who, in turn, will offer them at the appropriate moment to the left-arm manipulator who then makes them available on cue, by means of the puppet's left hand, to the head puppeteer. The unseen junior puppeteer sees to it that the prop is returned to the prop room after use. In another scene, the same junior puppeteer may have a brief appearance alone as a tsume, reappearing soon thereafter as a leg operator. As leg operator, he knows that he must carry the chief puppeteer's stage clogs to the appropriate spot so that the left-arm manipulator can position them properly for his senior to mount before making his appearance on stage. Memorizing relevant portions of the kowaricho is thus as vital to puppeteers of every level as memorizing every word of the script itself and the music to which it is spoken or sung. The cue book records not only who is on stage in what capacity but also signals puppeteers their location in the wings while waiting, stage entrances and exits for actual stage appearances as well as for those presences on stage which are hidden from the audience.

"A puppeteer really has only ten peak years," says Kanjuro, as he slides his right hand into the right kimono sleeve of a large male doll to see if he has tied its arm on at the proper length. "By the time you're fifty-five, you should have everything under enough control so that you feel confident on stage. By that time you will have mastered all the basic techniques, worked out your own style, perfected some roles, had experience in many others. But it takes until your fifties before you're really any good as a puppeteer. Between fifty-five and sixty-five, your knowledge and your body will be apt to be in balance. You know what to do and how to do it, and your body has the strength and fluidity to do it properly. Until then, you're too young, you wobble, you're uncertain or awkward, or have rough spots. After sixty-five, your body starts to deteriorate, your legs weaken, your hips are not as firm, your arms can't take those long stints of standing stock still on stage. Yes, it's a lifetime spent for ten good years.

"The head puppeteers who do all the male parts have the shortest life span in Bunraku, the tayu and the puppeteers specializing in female roles are next. The shamisen players live the longest."

Kanjuro's childhood was one of poverty and hard work. To alleviate his loneliness as he was shuttled back and forth among relatives, he took all sorts of odd jobs, from selling rice cakes before breakfast to storytelling with posters after school.

"I ended up in Osaka where the man next door had a job making sets for the old Bunraku theatre. He figured I could use a job. One day he marched me off and took me in to see Monjuro, the puppeteer. And suddenly there I was, twelve years old and apprenticed to Monjuro who was thirty-one. I was with him until he died in 1970 at the age of seventy—by then he was a 'living national treasure.'

"Those were good years with Monjuro. Sure, he used to scold me, even hit me now and then, but I'll never forget those first few years. Some of the best times were even before I got to use the legs—hours watching from the wings, fetching props, listening, absorbing the words unconsciously.

"Monjuro taught me the importance of an entrance—within those first minutes on stage, the puppeteer must establish the doll's identity, character, and emotions and convey the meaning of the role.

"As a leg manipulator, you learn to do the kata, the poses and stylized types of walks, strides, stances of horror or surprise or triumph. These kata must become automatic—you must move without giving the separate movements a thought.

"I like those big puppets with lots of movement, although there are scenes when the doll must be held motionless on stage for thirty or forty minutes. Some of those scenes are absolutely excruciating—my arms ache or even become completely numb.

"I like good supporting roles too, like old fathers. Those puppets are usually very light, and the trick is to move so that the dolls appear heavy with grief, suffering, or fear. In a comic part like Gihei in *Katsuragawa*, the problem is to get the audience laughing—if you try too hard for a laugh, you'll never get it. Sure, Bunraku has a lot of slapstick and broad comedy but even that has to be carefully done. And the puppeteer himself must keep an absolutely straight face—if I laugh when Gihei guffaws at runny-nosed Chokichi, the comic effect of Gihei's actions is ruined.

"Roles in which a hara-kiri is involved are particularly difficult because I go through all the pain of anticipating the disembowelment, then suffering through it while trying to give the part the artistic and dramatic quality it requires. After all, a man with his belly cut open could not converse for half an hour as characters do in Bunraku, so this dying business is tough to work out."

Kanjuro seats himself and writes several pages in the cue book, moving his tongue between his lips in concentration as his brush forms the special, stylized characters. His calligraphic skill makes him the natural choice to write the cue books.

"They say that three days on stage or three days as a beggar on the streets and you're hooked for life. I think that's right—I've never thought of quitting the Bunraku world. It's a very different world, this little Bunraku society of ours. It's no way to make a fortune. The hours are long, and we're away from home a lot. But it is satisfying, worthwhile, and always different. I'm very fortunate.''

Minotaro, Kanjuro's son, is a promising young puppeteer who originally had no intention of following in his father's footsteps. He came to the theatre to assist his father as a dutiful son on a part-time basis but he soon found himself immersed in the puppet world. Looking back on having joined the troupe at the age of fourteen, Minotaro emphasizes the importance of learning to operate tsume, the one-man puppets, well.

"People seem to think that a tsume is unimportant and that learning to move one is child's play for anyone but that is simply not true. The way a tsume walks on stage must first of all convey his social status—is he an important messenger from a daimyo or samurai, or is he just a village constable? Is the female servant a comic lady-in-waiting at court or is she a maid in the licensed quarters? The pace and posture must reveal the person's character and state of mind also. The agitation of an imperial messenger reporting the impending visit of a court minister or the farmer's fear that his son will be mistaken for a noble child whose head must be borne to the ruler, as in *Sugawara Denju,* have to be conveyed quickly in the tsume's short walk-on part. Farmers and clerks, maids and ladies-in-waiting walk differently. It's really true that a man who can't move a tsume convincingly will never make a good puppeteer. Using tsume is important training for use of the hands and arms, teaching a puppeteer how the use of his body is translated into puppet movements. Using a tsume really is basic training, not only in movement but also in learning the script, the entire play.''

Although Minotaro's initial training was with his father, he was assigned to Minosuke, a leading manipulator of female puppets, for apprenticeship. "Those years of concentrated practice with the legs were not easy but they are so important,'' the enthusiastic young man reports. "I would tie the cotton-stuffed practice legs together and work with them hung around my neck. Practicing leg movements holding onto the heel grips, working out the number and length of steps required to move the legs but to keep out of the head puppeteer's way, crouched way down but with my wrists at his hip level and turning quickly without holding him back—that takes terrific concentration and lots of solitary practice, often in front of a mirror, to say nothing of memorizing the play.

"And all that foot-stamping the leg operator must do made my feet red and tender and painful. But being stiff or sore is never an excuse for not continuing. Our seniors say they can always tell if a puppeteer has practiced well on his own. It shows up in his work, and disciplined training using a tsume and all types of legs determines the skill a puppeteer will display later as a head puppeteer." Even today, the promise seen in a junior puppeteer is inevitably attributed by his seniors to dedicated and intensive self-discipline and training, a good ten years, with tsume and legs.

At seventy-two, Kamematsu is the oldest puppeteer in the troupe. His round face is unlined except for the furrows that appear in his brow when he concentrates on movements of his puppet. "When I joined Bunraku, I worked from early in the morning until late at night and thought nothing of it. In those first years, I'd go off to the theatre with my box lunch and then come home with it still untouched, and my mother kept saying that it was a disgrace to be working with an outfit that didn't even give you time to eat. But frankly, I was so busy that I don't remember ever being hungry."

Although Kamematsu complains of a certain loss of strength in his legs these days, his handling of puppets is disciplined and elegant. His ability to remain expressionless in emotional roles makes him almost invisible behind the animated puppet.

"I went to primary school with the daughter of Bungoro, the puppeteer who performed until he died at ninety-three," Kamematsu recalls, speaking very quickly. "When I was eleven, I walked to the theatre with her one afternoon to take her father an umbrella. Bungoro insisted that I come to work for him as an apprentice. In those first years, I did everything—helped with props, did errands, moved scenery, watched, finally got to manipulate legs. Since I was the only youngster in the group, I was kept on the run all day. Severe treatment was not unusual in those days. Why, they'd set the cops on you nowadays if you slapped a young leg operator!

"I've been in work that I've liked for six decades and have never thought of quitting. There's never an unpleasant day and never a day when I don't think I can do better if I just keep at it. If a puppeteer ever thinks he's got it down pat, he's finished. This is a 'not yet, but soon' type of career. Discipline, training, practice. There's always something ahead to work for." Kamematsu shifts his stocky body and looks in the mirror to arrange a few thin strands of hair carefully across his head. "That rainy day that took me to the Bunraku theatre in 1916 changed my life. But there's more to do, lots more."

Itcho, Kamematsu's son, who joined his father as a puppeteer at the age of seventeen in 1955, appears at the dressing room door. Father and son walk down the hall without a word.

"It's a good feeling to know you'll be a member of the group all your life," says Juzo, the shamisen player who was born in 1899. "We stay together and are always part of the Bunraku community. You don't get tossed out to retirement at fifty-five. You have a place until you die."

At eighteen, Seinosuke is the youngest puppeteer in the troupe. "I joined Bunraku at twelve because I liked it," says the Tokyo lad. "I still do." He carries himself with confidence, but he watches to be sure he complies strictly with the etiquette.

Although many of the graduates (totaling twenty-four men as of May 1984) of the formal Bunraku course sponsored by the national theatres of Tokyo and Osaka have proved reliable and competent puppeteers, tayu, and musicians, there is still strong prejudice, seldom articulated, against them by the members of the troupe who joined at a younger age and survived the rigors of unplanned training. The latter sometimes remark, "Those guys are too old. Their bodies have already hardened and their heads are full of strange ideas. They don't know how to fit in properly, they don't show proper respect for the years we've put into Bunraku, and they ask too many questions. Always why. What is important is how, not why, results, not theories. They should learn with their bodies and not always be scribbling down notes."

The results of the intensive training course will not be known for decades. Daily demonstrations and lessons by puppeteers, narrators, and musicians who take turns conscientiously teaching the young recruits can bring them quickly to a fairly high technical level. "But Bunraku is more than technique," says a senior member of the troupe. "Training the hands, the feet, the lungs, the hips is only a part of Bunraku. More important is training the spirit."

In speaking of some of the young musicians, an older performer commented, "They can play the notes, the melodies all right. Their rhythm is correct but the notes are dead. They play 'cheen, cheen,' but it should be 'cheeeen, cheeeen' played with feeling so that you feel it in your hara. The trouble is some of these young shamisen players think all they have to do is learn the fingering. They don't play from their own hara." Another man chimed in, "Not only that, but they appear out from behind the bamboo blinds too soon. Once on the yuka, they start to think they're hot stuff before they know anything more than rudimentary techniques." The first man continued, "That's true of some tayu also. When they start out, they yell. A loud voice doesn't make gidayu convincing and they should remain hidden until they learn to project their voices instead of just howling. Oh yes, there are some good young guys coming out of that school—I could even name them—but it's not right when they start looking down their noses at those of us who slaved our way up the rungs by learning, not by being taught in some fancy training school."

Rehearsing has always required close cooperation between three puppeteers —or sometimes six, when two puppets are used to polish the action in specific scenes. A tayu and shamisen player, or a group of four or five of each category will join for several rehearsals prior to the two days of dress rehearsals, or *butai geiko* (literally, "stage practice"), that precede opening day of an Osaka or Tokyo run. By the time butai geiko takes place, each performer is responsible for knowing his part thoroughly. Should a leg operator move too slowly, he will be told so by the left-arm manipulator as well as the head puppeteer. From the wings, an older head puppeteer will also suddenly materialize on stage to push the young man, hands on shoulders, through a neater turn. A puppeteer senior to that head puppeteer will chime in and call out a rhythm or a cue word or two, saying, "That's when you must start the turn," and at this stage even Tamao is apt to enter the coaching session by suggesting that the trio move closer to center stage. The young leg manipulator is expected to accept and absorb all this advice as constructive criticism, as friendly assistance, even should it be barked at him in strong terms. There is no room for young temperaments or hurt feelings in Bunraku rehearsals. Some young performers confide that the only way they can receive helpful instruction is by knowingly making a mistake that prompts a senior to demonstrate the correct movement, but such a ruse can only occasionally be employed without incurring the senior's ire or suspicion.

The closeness of the Bunraku troupe is a result of the strict code of behavior, disciplined training, entire lifetimes devoted to repertory performance, and even a special secret language. Graduates of the excellently planned training course often find it hard to strike the balance between establishing close ties, which combine features of a family and those of a profession, and maintaining a respectful distance. The borderline between familiarity and convention is unmarked in the Bunraku world, but the conventions must be followed.

Entering Bunraku is a commitment for life, and it is fairly unusual for men to leave. In some cases, a performer will suddenly feel that the financial and psychological pressure of maintaining a family of four on a salary of less than a thousand dollars a month after some fifteen years of experience is simply beyond him. Occasionally, a member of the troupe finds slow progress through the ranks, an unusually strict or perhaps slightly inattentive master, or the restricted life with demanding hours simply intolerable after several years, and once in a while a young man discovers or is helped to discover that he is simply not suited for the way of Bunraku. The weak link disappears. The remaining members of the troupe join ranks, and the chain of support and discipline soon repairs itself.

Bunraku flourishes because of long, slow nourishment, late flowering, and careful reseeding. Tradition, discipline, and lifetime dedication make it possible for the small Bunraku community to continue to create a unique theatrical experience.

In 1984, Koshijidayu became seventy-one and there were by then three other "living national treasures" (Tsudayu, Tamao, and Kanjuro). Komatsudayu became fifty-two. Kamematsu's fifteen-year-old grandson (Itcho's son) became the second third-generation performer in the troupe (and also the youngest), due to complete the National Bunraku Theatre's training course in April 1985; like his father and grandfather, who became seventy-nine in 1984, he is a puppeteer. Tamao's grandson started training with Tamao in 1983, his official apprenticeship as a puppeteer starting in 1985 (Tamao's son works in a field unrelated to Bunraku). Mojitayu turned sixty in 1984, and assumption of his late father's name, Sumitayu, is scheduled for April 1985. Juzo became eighty-five in 1984 and is carried on the troupe's rolls as a non-performing musician who teaches and advises.

In the new Osaka theatre, all fourteen dressing rooms are on the second floor, behind the backstage area. The wig master, repairer of heads, costume director, and seamstress work on the third floor where there is also a large storage room for props.

Training school classrooms and small rehearsal rooms are on the fourth floor. Officials of the Bunraku Association and the National Bunraku Theatre of Osaka occupy many rooms on various floors. Compilation of records and research relating to Bunraku are handled by numerous officials of both groups. Detailed volumes pertaining to specific plays, authors, performances, etc., (*Joen Shiryoshu*, in Japanese only) and programs (in Japanese and English) are issued for each Osaka and Tokyo run.

On March 24, 1985, shamisen player Enza was designated a "living national treasure.

On Tour

8:50 a.m. Dwarfed by the towering stone wall that four centuries ago was part of a castle moat, a long truck is parked up against the wide unloading platform of a modern community hall in a village in Shikoku. A group of young men in chinos and jeans, stagehands from the Asahi Theatre, begins to remove the tarpaulin that covers the cargo. They carry off the bamboo-framed burlap crates one by one, working in an orderly, brisk fashion, chatting and joking all the while. Each man knows exactly where each case goes and unloads it gently from his shoulder to place it in the wings or by a dressing room. The flats are the last to be unloaded. Pieces of the set of the "Terakoya" scene of *Sugawara Denju Tenarai Kagami*—a modest village house with a pile of schoolboys' desks painted on one wall, a stack of paper shoji, and a backdrop showing farmers' fields and thatched cottages—sway as they are set up in racks in the wings.

9:30 a.m. The stagehands start setting up the traditional Bunraku partitions and stage entrances with bits of lumber and parts of sets. Suzuki, naked from the waist up except for the wide knitted wool belly-band he wears even in summer, checks hallways and wings to make sure that each *bote,* the special burlap cases the troupe uses for all its tours, is in its proper place. With Ishibashi, the costume man, he sets up a stand for the puppets, two lengths of pipes fitted into A-frames of wood. From the pipes hang lengths of heavy twine with finger-size wooden sticks attached.

Suzuki removes a dozen pairs of stage clogs from a packing case. He checks each one to see that the straw sandals used to sole them are firmly tied on, and lines them up according to height. "Two, four, six . . ." he counts, and rubs the sweat from his brow when he reaches an odd number, muttering to himself as he stands up to retrieve the single tall clog he has been sitting on.

"Remember the time in Tokyo we had two clogs missing, one from each of the two pairs of different heights?" Ishibashi nods. "They had to fly the two odd clogs up from Osaka. You're just never sure until you unpack."

10:00 a.m. Leaning over another case, Ishibashi is unpacking headless puppets, which have been folded in two. The dangling feet clatter and thump together and legs sway and revolve below the kimono hems. Ishibashi inspects each puppet carefully and then slips it by the keyhole opening in its shoulder board onto the rope-hung bits of wood. The legs of the Matsuomaru doll, bulky in two layers of padded black velveteen embroidered in white and gold, twirl eerily a few inches above the floor.

In a small, matted room opening onto the area beyond the wings, Nakoshi is cheerfully setting up shop. From two cases, he removes each bulky round parcel carefully with two hands; he unties the enveloping yellow padded hoods one by one, and takes out the puppet heads, each with its hair meticulously dressed and combed. On the shelf he has made by standing his bote on their sides and padding them with a layer of folded head-protectors, Nakoshi lays out an array of kashira. There are the two Bunshichi heads for Matsuomaru, the noble warrior. Next to them are the two heads for Chiyo, his wife. There are strong Genzo, the schoolmaster, and his wife, Tonami, and an aristocratically coiffed woman's kashira next to that. Children's heads abound. Two are fine-featured, the other five humorous, rustic, less carefully delineated.

Nakoshi turns his puppet heads carefully, displaying them as neatly as the conscientious greengrocer displays his eggplants and cabbages. Nakoshi counts the unpacked objects and, satisfied, proceeds to remove the wads of newspaper from the massive sidelocks of several male dolls. He then drops crosslegged onto a cushion and sets up his battered hair-dressing stand. Fastening Matsuomaru's kashira into the bamboo holder, he uses a wide-toothed comb to adjust the heavy tuft of hair, the "one-hundred-days' growth."

Young puppeteers already in black cotton robes neatly tied at the right stop to select from Nakoshi's wares. He peers over his glasses proprietarily at each head as the men check the big and small toggles, inspect the coiffures, and depart with the heads they need after voicing or nodding thanks.

10:30 a.m. Puppeteer Bunjaku comes to Nakoshi's stand, and they decide that

Tonami's hair should be smoothed a bit. Tamao stops on his way to inspect the progress on stage and requests that Matsuomaru's left eyebrow be trimmed. The men raise their voices to be heard over the hammering that comes from the stage.

"They're going to use empty beer cases to get the stage partitions up to the right level," laughs a young puppeteer. "The stagehands say that's the only way they can get the house area up high enough to make a proper stage for us to work on." Nakoshi shrugs, and the junior puppeteer goes on stage to check the height of the partitions against his body.

The old offstage musician with the bushy eyebrows is unpacking his flutes and drums assisted by the young drummer. They pull over a table and two chairs, spread out some wrapping cloths, and quickly have their instruments in order. "It won't sound the same being on the same level with the stage, but at least it's cooler down here," says the gray-haired man, mopping his forehead.

Near the assemblage of seated drums, the prop man is pounding nails to construct a child's writing desk for the first scene. He finishes it and goes over to the grand piano, abandoned in the far wings, on whose black cloth cover he has already laid out the swords, shroud box, head box with the attached child's head, and glass rosaries in the order in which they will be used by the puppeteers.

At the other side of the stage, Kashiwagi is supervising placement of the platform on which the tayu and musician will perform, since revolving side stages are a standard theatre fixture in only one city in Shikoku. He lines up the narrators' lecterns in order of use and then beats the cushions to puff them up properly for the narrators' and musicians' comfort.

11:00 a.m. The entrance to the puppeteers' dressing room is paved with zori. The men go to the hall to retrieve bundles from the packing cases there. The cloth-wrapped parcels are opened up, and each man brings out a set or two of puppet arms, a sewing kit, a dog-eared script, and his own neatly folded stage outfit, some the simple black side-tied robe, some the kimono and formal kamishimo to go over it.

Around the matted room, eighteen men are unpacking and laying out their dressing-table runners, their mirrors and combs, their photographs and amulets. The room is strewn with their personal floor cushions, some with green crocheted borders, a few of silken sheen, some hand-embroidered with flowers or initials or decorated with a lace frill. The men amble around the room as they put on their white or black tabi, white or black tights, and black cotton robes. Some are winding their arms up in cotton gloves, others are stepping into hakama.

11:30 a.m. Seijuro takes a pair of arms out to the puppet rack and taps the doll he dressed ten days ago in Osaka. He eyes it casually up and down as it turns in a slow, ghostly dance. He adjusts a neckband, pats the shoulders into shape, then ties on the arms. He wanders casually to the stage, where he and Bunjaku silently measure their first entrances, deciding where the first pose will take place, and gauging exactly how high the improvised stage-rear section has been raised.

11:45 a.m. In another dressing room there is a thump as a tayu drops his hara obi on the tatami. It unwinds like so much fire hose, and the man turns to open his cotton kimono and binds himself up for his performance. The wings of his costume crackle as he tosses them over his kimono.

"I used to like stones in my otoshi," says a colleague as he slips the long pillow into his kimono. "Now that I've gained weight, this one filled with dried red beans feels better."

Another tayu tosses his otoshi lightly with one hand. "It's really what you *think* feels right. I've used sand and tiny stones for twenty years and the mixture still feels right against my body and in my hands."

11:55 a.m. The men stand as Tsudayu enters the room. He looks rested and happy after the toast and coffee he shared in the hotel dining room with his son, Midoridayu, and Kichibei, the shamisen player who will perform with him. "It looks like a nice modern theatre," he says pleasantly as he starts to change his clothes.

Kichibei buffs his well-shaped pate with a handkerchief, then settles down to tune and play his shamisen. "It takes a good hour to get the right tone," he says as he removes a dented tin case from a scarred, old-fashioned leather suitcase. He extracts a square wooden shamisen soundbox and proceeds to fit the three joints of the neck into it and to tie on and adjust the strings. Next to him sits Dohachi, another shamisen player, a pitch pipe in his mouth, his eyes closed like a placid god in meditation. He plucks at the yellow silk strings, and the wooden tuning pegs squeak as he turns them.

At a respectful distance and with his eyes to the wall, young Seitomo also works on his shamisen, but he has draped a cotton cloth over the strings, and his plectrum makes muted, barely audible sounds. "Not to disturb them," he murmurs as he bends over to check his box of bridges.

12:00 noon. Downstairs on stage, the set is up. Stagehands wander about. They are now in their black Bunraku tunics and wearing their black hoods with the front flaps flicked up over their foreheads until curtain time at one o'clock. Young puppeteers take up their posts by various entrances to the set, some watching over a prop, several waiting with stage clogs of various heights. Young puppeteer Minoshi stands with a black-kimonoed figure of Chiyo, her aristocratic head now in place, draped across his arms as he waits for Kamematsu and his son, Itcho.

12:45 p.m. Puppeteer Tamame picks up the ebony sticks from the prop man and readies himself to strike the *ni cho,* the two whacks before the curtain is opened that signal that everyone is in place. Minosuke sits in the wings with the tsuke, the light wooden sticks he will strike on a board on the floor at climactic moments during the play that is about to start. Only an experienced puppeteer is entrusted with sounding the tsuke in the dramatically important passages of the "Terakoya" scene.

Aioidayu is in his place behind his lectern, his face serious and serene without the puckish smile that distinguishes him offstage. Seitomo sits next to him, his shamisen now unshrouded.

12:55 p.m. On stage, the junior puppeteers are in place with their child puppets already acting at practicing their calligraphy in the village classroom. The drums and flutes sound the overture.

1:00 p.m. The clappers give a resounding crack, and in a town on the island of Shikoku, population 30,000, the curtain opens on *Sugawara Denju.*

Aioidayu and Seitomo present the fifteen-minute introductory portion of the scene. The tayu changes his voice to portray the six children, the school-master's wife Tonami, the mother who comes to enroll her son, the new scholar, and a merry servant who accompanies them. Bamboo blinds are dropped in front of the makeshift yuka and Aioidayu and Seitomo leave. To the sounds of flutes and drums played offstage, Tsudayu and Kichibei take their places, and the blinds are rolled up to reveal them seated and ready. A hooded pup-peteer announces the next portion of the scene and introduces Tsudayu and Kichibei. Tsudayu lifts the thick libretto to his forehead and bows again. Kichibei adjusts the shamisen and strikes a note, then several more.

1:15 p.m. In a calm resonant voice, his long fingers carefully positioned on his knees, Tsudayu sets the scene.

The curtain rings make their characteristic rasp as the black cloth is whipped open then snapped shut to allow Seijuro to enter, operating the puppet Genzo. Even on tour, the troupe uses its regular black stage-entrance curtains marked in white, the crests always a silent reminder of the rivalry of two important figures in Osaka puppetry who, almost three centuries ago, set Bunraku on the path it follows today.

The schoolmaster Genzo enters slowly and is greeted by Tonami, who in-troduces the new student. Genzo is surprised at his aristocratic voice and bear-ing, but he sends the boys off to play.

Tsudayu throws himself into the roles as the play reaches its first climax. As Genzo and Tonami agree they must kill the new student in order to save the lord's son they are hiding, the air is filled with tension. Tsudayu's voice conveys the schoolmaster's horror as he recognizes his duty, and the fear that grips his wife's heart at what must be done.

The geza musicians make ominous sounds as the large puppet portraying cruel Gemba stamps onto the stage.

In the wings, Tamao is on an unusually high pair of stage clogs waiting for the cue for the important entrance of Matsuomaru. Tamasho, hooded, holds the rod of the puppet's left hand, his fingers taut and steady at the side of the thirty-eight pound puppet. *"O-o-rai!"* says Tamao in a loud stage whisper, and the two maneuver the huge doll onto the stage, Tamame crouching below to work the legs in a wide gait and to stamp his own feet repeatedly.

Tsudayu's face is now a network of rivulets of perspiration and his face is contorted as he portrays Matsuomaru, who must identify the head of an executed child as the son of his former lord; Gemba, who has come to see that the cruel order is obeyed; Genzo, who must kill an innocent child to protect the child who is being sought; and Tonami, the terrified wife. Some comedy is injected into the scene for the next ten minutes as five children are fetched by their fathers and grandfathers, played by one-man tsume puppets, leaving only the hidden child and the new student on stage. Tsudayu recites the dialogue of fourteen people in this section. Kichibei strums merrily along to enliven the scene before the drama of the climax ahead.

Backstage, the prop man is already disassembling the desks used in the first part of the scene and packing them into cases with the writing sets. Ishibashi packs the student dolls into another basket, but their heads have already been wrapped by Nakoshi and tucked into the bottom of his packing case.

Action continues on stage: Slamming the tsuke on their board, Minosuke signals one climax, then another, as Tsudayu narrates the horror of the innocent child's killing, mercifully out of sight, and the breathtaking suspense as Matsuomaru inspects the head and identifies it for wicked Gemba as that of the wanted child. Matsuomaru's son has been sacrificed knowingly by his father in order to save the child of the statesman to whom he once gave fealty and to whom he remains secretly loyal; the scene is a poignant tangle of conflicting emotions. Sacrifice, loyalty, parental love, suspicion, hidden grief, gratitude for having been allowed to participate in the sacrifice are all portrayed by the voice of the tayu accented by a few notes of the shamisen, and by the puppets whose very expressions change with the angle of the head, the gestures of the arms, and the carriage of the body.

In the wings Tamao gives the heavy doll in embroidered robes to a junior puppeteer and returns on stage with an entirely different Matsuomaru puppet. The head is slightly smaller, the costume of plain black silk. Another dramatic scene ensues as Matsuomaru joins his wife, the grieving mother of the slain child, and urges her to rejoice with him at the successful sacrifice of their brave son.

Once again Tamao leaves the stage with his puppet, followed by Kamematsu operating the puppet Chiyo. There is an orderly scramble behind the stage-rear entrance as Tamao is assisted in moving the Matsuomaru head into a costumed form in white mourning clothes and as Kamematsu exchanges the Chiyo doll he has been using for one attired, like Matsuomaru, in white garments and with a slightly smaller head. The first Chiyo puppet is removed by a young assistant. By the time Tamao and Kamematsu are back on stage performing the moving and graceful dance of lamentation that brings the scene to an end, Ishibashi is packing the first Matsuomaru and Chiyo puppets into a case, making sure that they are placed so that the costumes will be minimally disarranged before use tomorrow in the next town.

2:35 p.m. The clappers sound the end of the play; the curtain is drawn. Tsudayu steps down from his lectern and Kichibei follows. They turn to each other. Bowing, they thank each other formally: "*Arigato gozaimashita.*" They walk to the dressing rooms.

In the puppeteers' dressing room the air is lively as the men reroll their cloth bundles of doll limbs, drop their toilet articles into small bags, and dress in sport shirts and casual trousers.

The shamisens are put back in their case. Aioidayu has perched his straw hat on the back of his head, and his smile reappears. Tsudayu straightens his striped necktie. The old geza man ties a final knot on the bote of drums. Nakoshi combs his hair and starts to whistle.

3:30 p.m. A sleek new bus draws up at the stage entrance. The performers climb on, younger men last. The bus drives off with thirty-seven members of the Osaka Bunraku Troupe, leaving only a few stagehands to load the truck and catch up with the bus contingent at the inn in the next town on the tour.

4:00 p.m. "Good house today," says Suzuki, packing stage clogs.

"Yes, they liked it all right. They cried," says a carpenter tugging at a nail.

The Bunraku Troupe tours Japan with increasing frequency and to larger and more enthusiastic audiences. Although Tamasho, Kichibei, Dohachi, and Seijuro have died since this account was written in 1977, other performers have developed their skills and continue to grow in artistic strength. Many younger men have joined the troupe. Tours continue to combine busy, tiring appearances in new theatres and lively intervals of camaraderie. Tours abroad are also more numerous as people of other cultures discover the fascination of Bunraku, Japan's unique form of puppet drama that has proven itself capable of transcending language barriers around the world.

APPENDICES

Members of the Osaka Bunraku Troupe

Performers

First Name	Last Name	Function	Year of Birth	Age (1985)	Entered Bunraku: Year	Age
Aioidayū	Takemoto	Narrator	1939	46	1953	24
Asazō	Tsuruzawa	Shamisen player	1950	35	1972*	22
Bunjaku	Yoshida	Puppeteer	1928	57	1945	17
Bungo	Yoshida	Puppeteer	1934	51	1951	17
Bunshō	Yoshida	Puppeteer	1931	54	1944	23
Chitosedayū	Takemoto	Narrator	1959	26	1977	19
Danji	Takezawa	Shamisen player	1960	25	1978*	18
Danroku VIII	Takezawa	Shamisen player	1928	57	1943	15
Danshichi	Takezawa	Shamisen player	1935	50	1953	18
Datejidayū	Takemoto	Narrator	1928	57	1946	18
Enjirō	Tsuruzawa	Shamisen player	1959	26	1977*	18
Enza **	Tsuruzawa	Shamisen player	1914	71	1925	11
Fukumaru	Yoshida	Puppeteer	1941	44	1955	14
Hachisuke	Tsuruzawa	Shamisen player	1952	33	1974*	22
Hanafusadayū	Toyotake	Narrator	1947	38	1968	21
Hidetama	Yoshida	Puppeteer	1957	28	1979*	22
Ichisuke	Kiritake	Puppeteer	1969	16	1983	14
Itchō	Kiritake	Puppeteer	1938	47	1955	17
Jūzō IV	Tsuruzawa	Shamisen player	1899	86	1911	12
Kameji	Kiritake	Puppeteer	1953	32	1974*	21
Kamematsu IV	Kiritake	Puppeteer	1905	80	1916	11
Kan'ichi	Kiritake	Puppeteer	1963	22	1983*	20
Kanju	Kiritake	Puppeteer	1945	40	1955	10

*Entered the two-year Bunraku training program at the National Theatre.
**A "living national treasure."

Kanjūrō **	Kiritake	Puppeteer	1920	65	1932	12
Kanotarō	Tsuruzawa	Shamisen player	1904	81	1913	9
Kanroku	Kiritake	Puppeteer	1955	30	1977*	22
Kan'ya	Kiritake	Puppeteer	1955	30	1974*	19
Katsuhei	Nozawa	Shamisen player	1938	47	1950	12
Katsutarō II	Nozawa	Shamisen player	1912	73	1924	12
Kazusuke	Yoshida	Puppeteer	1960	25	1980*	20
Kazuo	Yoshida	Puppeteer	1947	38	1967	20
Kinshi IV	Nozawa	Shamisen player	1917	68	1951	34
Kin'ya	Nozawa	Shamisen player	1957	28	1976*	19
Komatsudayū	Toyotake	Narrator	1932	53	1954	22
Komon	Kiritake	Puppeteer	1927	58	1940	13
Koshijidayū IV**	Takemoto	Narrator	1913	72	1924	11
Kōsuke	Yoshida	Puppeteer	1966	19	1980	14
Matsukadayū	Toyotake	Narrator	1941	44	1959	18
Midoridayū	Takemoto	Narrator	1950	35	1965	15
Minoichirō	Yoshida	Puppeteer	1958	27	1980	22
Minojirō	Yoshida	Puppeteer	1954	31	1976*	22
Minosuke III	Yoshida	Puppeteer	1933	52	1940	7
Minotarō	Yoshida	Puppeteer	1953	32	1967	14
Miwatayū	Takemoto	Narrator	1946	39	1971	25
Mojiedayū	Takemoto	Narrator	1946	39	1972*	26
Mojihisadayū	Takemoto	Narrator	1955	30	1980*	25
Monju	Kiritake	Puppeteer	1934	51	1950	16
Nambudayū V	Takemoto	Narrator	1916	69	1930	14
Nanjudayū	Takemoto	Narrator	1965	20	1982*	17
Nantodayū	Takemoto	Narrator	1955	30	1980*	25
Nanshidayū	Takemoto	Narrator	1949	36	1972*	23
Oritayū V	Takemoto	Narrator	1932	53	1946	14
Orimidayū	Takemoto	Narrator	1959	26	1980*	21
Rodayū V	Toyotake	Narrator	1945	40	1952	7
Sakitayū	Toyotake	Narrator	1944	41	1953	9
Sakujūrō	Yoshida	Puppeteer	1920	65	1935	15
Seigo	Tsuruzawa	Shamisen player	1967	18	1983	16
Seigorō	Toyomatsu	Narrator	1960	25	1980*	20
Seiji	Tsuruzawa	Shamisen player	1945	40	1953	8
Seijirō	Tsuruzawa	Shamisen player	1965	20	1978	13
Seinosuke	Toyomatsu	Puppeteer	1958	27	1971	13
Seisuke	Tsuruzawa	Shamisen player	1952	33	1968	16
Seitomo	Tsuruzawa	Shamisen player	1947	38	1971	24
Seizaburō	Toyomatsu	Puppeteer	1957	28	1977*	20

Shimatayū	Toyotake	Narrator	1932	53	1948	16
Sumitayū VII	Takemoto	Narrator	1924	61	1946	22
Takatayū	Takemoto	Narrator	1948	37	1971	23
Tamae	Yoshida	Puppeteer	1950	35	1974*	24
Tamagorō II	Yoshida	Puppeteer	1910	75	1925	15
Tamaka	Yoshida	Puppeteer	1966	19	1983*	17
Tamaki	Yoshida	Puppeteer	1947	38	1972*	25
Tamakō	Yoshida	Puppeteer	1938	47	1952	14
Tamamatsu	Yoshida	Puppeteer	1933	52	1947	14
Tamame	Yoshida	Puppeteer	1953	32	1969	15
Tamanosuke	Yoshida	Puppeteer	1927	58	1943	16
Tamao **	Yoshida	Puppeteer	1919	66	1933	14
Tamashi	Yoshida	Puppeteer	1956	29	1977*	21
Tamaya	Yoshida	Puppeteer	1945	40	1971	26
Tamayo	Yoshida	Puppeteer	1969	16	1983	13
Tokutayū	Toyotake	Narrator	1931	54	1950	19
Tomisuke	Nozawa	Shamisen player	1955	30	1971	16
Tsudayū **	Takemoto	Narrator	1916	69	1924	8
Tsukomadayū	Takemoto	Narrator	1949	36	1969	20
Tsukunidayū	Takemoto	Narrator	1949	36	1972*	23
Tsumaidayū	Takemoto	Narrator	1959	26	1973	29
Wakatama	Yoshida	Puppeteer	1956	29	1975	19
Yasaburō	Takezawa	Shamisen player	1949	36	1972*	23

Urakata

First Name	Last Name	Function	Year of Birth
Kōji	Hishida	Keeper of heads	1936
Osamu	Ishibashi	Costume director	1936
Takayuki	Kashiwagi	Stage assistant	1931
Haruo	Mochizuki	Offstage musician	1941
Taishirō	Mochizuki	Offstage musician	1907
Shōji	Nakoshi	Wig master	1930
Kōji	Suzuki	Stage assistant	1947
Tsuruko	Uehara	Seamstress	1915
Tokiyo	Wada	Prop master	1931

Minosuke Ōe, though not an official member of the Bunraku troupe, carves all the puppet heads used in Bunraku. He was born in 1907.

The Bunraku Stage

The performance area of the Bunraku stage is approximately thirty-nine feet wide by just over fifteen feet deep. Its outstanding characteristic is the sunken stage area called the funazoko, or "ship's bottom." This important performance area, extending the full width of the stage and beyond the stage-entrance curtains into the wings, is approximately seven feet deep and is recessed fourteen inches below the stage level.

The funazoko is hidden from the audience by three stage partitions, the *tesuri*. The partition nearest the audience, *ichi no tesuri,* unfinished or painted matte black, runs across the very front of the forestage at a height of just over ten inches. Beyond this first partition are the footlights and the main stage curtain, which is drawn by

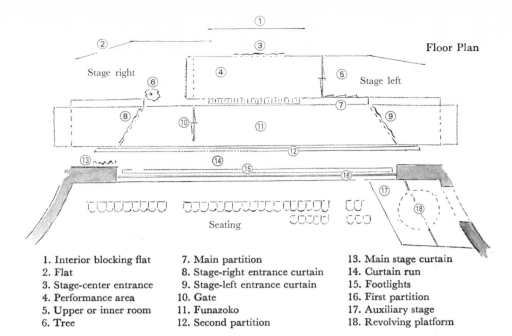

Floor Plan

Stage right

Stage left

Seating

1. Interior blocking flat
2. Flat
3. Stage-center entrance
4. Performance area
5. Upper or inner room
6. Tree

7. Main partition
8. Stage-right entrance curtain
9. Stage-left entrance curtain
10. Gate
11. Funazoko
12. Second partition

13. Main stage curtain
14. Curtain run
15. Footlights
16. First partition
17. Auxiliary stage
18. Revolving platform

a partially hidden stagehand who pulls it open toward the wings, stage right, by running across the forestage, an area which is never used for performance. The second stage partition, *ni no tesuri,* extends almost nineteen inches above the forestage and stands directly in front of the funazoko. This second partition is usually painted a neutral color to blend with the set. Upstage, behind the funazoko, stands the main set. It is erected at normal stage level and usually represents a house, shop, palace, or other interior space. The forward flat of the set incorporates the third stage partition, the *hon tesuri.* Reaching a height of approximately thirty-three inches, this serves to hide the puppeteers sufficiently to make the puppets appear to walk or sit on the tatami floor of the room represented.

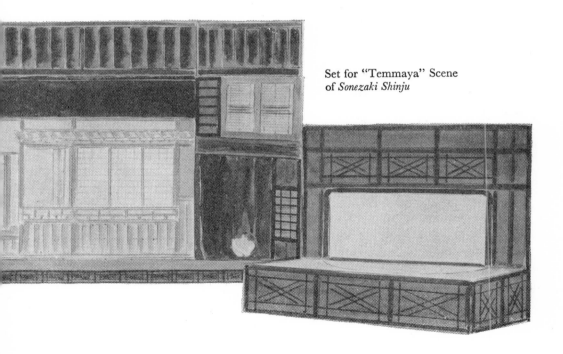

Set for "Temmaya" Scene
of *Sonezaki Shinju*

View of Stage Left

View of Stage Right

Glossary-Index

abdomen (*hara*): belly, gut; pit of the stomach; center of strength, emotions, and spiritual power, and particularly the source of a performer's ability, 57, 58, 61, 65–67, 157, 163; *see also* belly sash; suicide

Aioidayū IV (Takemoto), narrator, 72, 164–65, 167

amulets, 62, 163

animals, *see* props

apprentices (*deshi*) and apprenticeship: 9, 52, 78, 136, 137, 138, 148, 152, 154, 155; *see also* training

armature (*sashigane*): a device consisting of a wooden rod, a cord, and a lever attached to puppet's left arm; a puppeteer (left-arm manipulator) controls the cord with his right index and middle fingers; also attached to the right arm of puppets with articulated hands to be used by chief puppeteers, 3, 34, *36–37*, 117

arms, of puppets: 34, *36–37*, 93, 98, 117; acquisition by chief puppeteers, 117, 126; attachment to puppet, 124, 126, 128, 163

Asahi Theatre (Asahi-za), the Osaka theatre where Bunraku was performed from 1963 to 1984, xiii, 6, 7, 14, 93, 129, 132, 134–36

Asazō (Tsuruzawa), shamisen player, 73, 78

Ashiya Dōman Ōuchi Kagami (*The White Fox of Shinoda Wood*, 1734), historical play by Takeda Izumo, 8, 99, *139*

ashi-zukai, see leg operator

assistant, stage, *see* stage assistant

auditions, for training course, 9

auxiliary stage (*yuka*): small stage, incorporating a revolving circular platform, to the right (stage left) of the main stage on which narrators and musicians perform, 5, 10, 15, 30, 62, *67–72*; on tour, 162; *see also* shamisen players; *tayū*

Awaji: island east of Shikoku where puppetry has flourished since early times, 5

baba, see old woman

bachi, see plectrum

bag, narrators' (*otoshi*, "dropped thing"): a small (about four to nine inches long), homemade, cylindrical cloth bag or pillow containing beans, sand, stones, or a combination thereof that is slipped into the inside of the front of the kimono just above the sash and serves to keep the costume in place and to give the narrator something to grasp during his performance on stage, 61, 62, 163

baleen (*kujira no hige*): the horny substance growing in the mouth of filter-feeding whales and forming a fringelike sieve; dried and used to make springs for puppet heads, 97, *107*

balladeers, using *biwa* or fans, 3

bamboo blinds (*misu*): used to hide from the audience the offstage-musicians' room (*geza*) above the stage-right entrance curtain and the small room (*misuuchi*, "within the enclosure") above the stage-left entrance curtain in which the most junior tayu and shamisen players sometimes perform short scenes or portions of scenes, *20, 68, 74, 140–41*

bamboo hoops: inserted at the end of cloth strips hanging from the shoulder board of the puppet framework to represent the hips, *113*, 125

bamboo stands, for puppets, 31, 135; for puppet heads, 100, *109, 110*

bamboo toggles, *see* toggles

barefaced puppeteer (*de-zukai*): chief puppeteer who appears on stage unhooded, 10, 29; *see also* hoods

The Battles of Coxinga (*Kokusen'ya Kassen*, 1715), historical play by Chikamatsu Monzaemon, 8, *47*

beards, for puppets, 102, 103

beeswax, as hair dressing (*bintsuke*), 103

belly (*hara*), *see* abdomen

belly band (*hara maki*): knitted wool band worn over the abdomen as protection against chills and stomach problems, 160

belly sash (*hara obi*): supporting inner sash (obi), usually of heavy linen or cotton, worn by narrators, most sham-

isen players, and, of a different type, by puppeteers under their kimonos or performing robes, 61, 163

beni, benibana, see red dye; safflower

bintsuke, see beeswax

birds: calls, 84–85; as props, *139*; *see also* offstage musicians; props

biwa (Japanese lute): instrument used by balladeers, usually blind monks (*biwa hōshi*), in the lyric recitation of epic narratives, particularly tales of the Heike clan, 3

bodies, of puppets (*dō*): made of a shoulder board (*kata ita*), from which hangs a cloth or heavy paper trunk, into the end of which is inserted a bamboo hoop to represent the hips, *113*, 124, 125

bote, see packing case

bridges (*koma*), for shamisen, 76, 77, 164

Bungo (Yoshida), puppeteer; formerly Kotama, 32–33

Bungorō III (Yoshida), puppeteer (1869–1962); also known by title Naniwa-no-Jō bestowed by the imperial family, ix, xiii, 53, 55, 91, 94, 127, 155

Bunjaku (Yoshida), puppeteer, 87–92, 100, 101, 151, 162

Bunraku, definition of term, vii, 5

Bunraku Association (Bunraku Kyōkai), 6, 87, 159

Bunrakuken I (Uemura), 5

Bunrakuken II (Uemura, 1813–73): Bunrakuken I's successor, who established several theatres, including, in 1871, the first Bunraku-za, vii, 7

Bunraku Theatre (Bunraku-za), 6, 8, 93; change of name, 6, 7

Bunraku troupe: leadership, 10; leaving, 158; split into two groups (Chinami-kai and Mitsuwa-kai), 6

Bunraku-za, *see* Bunraku Theatre

Bunshichi: the most important and largest type of male puppet head, with several variations, named after the character in the play *Otokodate Itsutsu Karigane* (1745), 55, *110*, 115, *145*, 161

Bunzaburō (Yoshida), puppeteer and playwright (d. 1760), 5

burlap packing case, *see* packing case

butai geta, *see* stage clogs

calligraphy, used in the role distribution book, 153

cape (*mino*): a fringe of hair used in making puppet wigs, named for its resemblance to traditional straw rain capes, 102–3, 105, 110; *see also* wigs

carver, of puppet heads, 93–99, 103–9, 117–18

carving tools, 94–97

casting roles, 150–52

cat hide or catskin, attached to sides of shamisen soundbox, 76

chanter, *see* narrator

Chikamatsu Monzaemon (1653–1725): Japan's most famous and important Bunraku and Kabuki playwright, viii, xii, 8, 11, 13, 24–25, 56, 57, 88; *see also Heike Nyogo no Shima*; *Kokusen'ya Kassen*; *Sonezaki Shinjū*

child puppet head (*koyaku*): type of head used for child roles, male (*otoko no koyaku*) and female (*onna no koyaku*), 89, 92, 161, 164

Chinami-kai, 6

Chiyo, character in *Sugawara Denju Tenarai Kagami*, 92, 122, 161, 164, 166–67

Chōemon, character in *Katsuragawa Renri no Shigarami*, xii, 95

choi, *see* toggles

Chōkichi, character in *Katsuragawa Renri no Shigarami*, 153

chōshi, *see* tunings, shamisen

Chōzō, character in *Sonezaki Shinjū*, 92

The Chronicles of Decline and Prosperity (*Hiragana Seisuiki*, 1739), historical play by Takeda Izumo et al., 93, 94

Chūshingura, see *Kanadehon Chūshingura*

clappers (*hyōshigi* or *ki*): a pair of hardwood sticks (usually ebony or blackwood) struck together to signal openings and ends of scenes, plays, or portions thereof, 15, *20*, 30; or struck twice (*ni chō*) to indicate to performers that the stage is ready for the curtain to open, 164; also *tsuke*, a pair of wooden sticks struck on a board laid on the stage floor to underline climaxes, accentuate poses, or call attention to specific action, and occasionally used to create sound effects, 164

clogs, stage, *see* stage clogs

collar, *see* neckband

competition, among troupe members, 66, 150

copper headband (*daigane*): wig base which is nailed to puppet heads and onto which hair is attached, 103, 104

cording, decorative, for puppet wigs, 102

cords, *see* toggles

costumes (*ishō*), *112–14*, 119–23; narrators, 15, 32, 61, *69–72*, 163; nobility, *114*; puppeteers, 10, *38–41*, 135, *146*, 161, 162–63; shamisen players, 10, 32, *71–72, 74*; size of puppets', 33, 121; slit in puppets', 121, 124; stagehands, 164;

courtesan (*keisei, oiran*): 57, 88; coiffure, 101, 102, 103; costumes for, 92, *112, 114*, 120, 125–26; *see also* Ohatsu

The Courtesan's Colorful Dance Robe (*Hade-sugata Onna Maiginu*, 1772), play by Takemoto Saburōbei et al.; a domestic tragedy about merchant Hanshichi, his wife Osono, and his lover Sankatsu, 120

crests, Takemoto and Toyotake, iv, 17, 165; *see also* stage-entrance curtains

crying, narrator's mastery of, 150

cue book (*tsukechō*), of narrators, 64; of offstage musicians, 84, 85; also used generally to refer to role-distribution book; *see also* role-distribution book; notebooks

Cultural Affairs Agency (of the Ministry of Education), 6

curtain, *see* door curtain; stage curtain; stage-entrance curtain

cushion, floor (*zabuton*), 15, 62, 163

cypress, Japanese (*hinoki*), 93, 99

Danjirō, *see* Danshichi

Danroku (Takezawa), shamisen player, 32

Danshichi (Takezawa), formerly Danjirō, *71, 75*

Darasuke: male puppet head named after character in *En no Gyōja Ōmine Zakura* (1751), 92, 95; *see also* Kuheiji

Dechi: male puppet head used for simple, comic apprentices, servants, clowns, 92

deshi, *see* apprentices and apprenticeship

distributor of heads (*kashirawari iin*): person who selects the puppet heads for roles, 87–91

dō, *see* bodies, of puppets

dōgushi, *see* headgrip

Dōhachi II (Tsuruzawa), shamisen player (1915–81), 164, 167

domestic dramas, *see* plays, domestic

domestic tragedies, *see* plays, domestic

door curtain (*noren*): short divided curtain often hung at upstage center entrance of the set, particularly in domestic dramas, *19–21,* 27

Dōtombori, Osaka entertainment district, xiii, 4, 7, 13–14, 18

dressing rooms, 7, 51, 61, *114,* 127, 128, 135, *146,* 158, 162

dress rehearsals, *see* rehearsals

drums: *kotsuzumi* and *ōtsuzumi*, played at shoulder level with the hand; *taiko,* placed on a low floor stand, and *ōdaiko,* hung from a waist-high stand, both played with sticks or mallets, 82–86

ears, of puppets, 95, 97

Eiza I (Yoshida), puppeteer (1872–1945), 53

entrance, of puppets, 153

Enza (Tsuruzawa), shamisen player, 32

etiquette, among troupe members, 134–37, 147

eyebrows, of puppets, 162; operation of, 34; painted on female puppets, 116; *see also* heads, puppet; toggles

face-protector: wire frame made by each puppeteer to keep the black face hood (*zukin*) off the puppeteer's face and at a distance from his eyes that allows him maximum visibility, 30, *139, 143*

family lines, of puppeteers, 148

father-in-law (*shūto*): type of puppet head, 89

feet, of puppeteers, 51, 54; of puppets, 34, 54, 98; *see also* legs

fingers, *see* hands

flats, *see* sets

flutes, 82–86

focal point, of puppeteers, 149

footgear, of puppets, 129

foot manipulator, *see* leg operator

foot-stamping, 51, 54, 155

The Forty-Seven Rōnin (*Kanadehon Chū-shingura*, 1748), historical play by Takeda Izumo et al.; one of the most famous and popular pieces in the Bunraku repertory, 56, 91

foxes, 130, 132, *139*

Fujinami Prop Company (Fujinami Ko-dōgu-ya), 132

fukeoyama (middle-aged or mature woman): type of puppet head, 88, 92; *see also* heads, female

funazoko ("ship's bottom"): sunken stage area, 7 ft. wide and 14 in. below floor level, used for staging street, garden, or entranceway scenes, 41

furi, see gesture

fushi, see melody

futozao shamisen (shamisen with a thick neck): shamisen used in Bunraku; *see also gidayū*-shamisen

gay quarters, *see* licensed quarters

Gemba, character in *Sugawara Denju Tenarai Kagami,* 92, 165–66

Genta: type of male puppet head named after hero of *Hiragana Seisuiki,* 88, 90–91, 92, 94

Genzō, character in *Sugawara Denju Tenarai Kagami,* 92, 95, 161, 165–67

gesso (*gofun*): a paste prepared by mixing ground shells with glue and used as a coating or white paint, 98, 111, 115, 117, 118

gesture (*furi*): puppet's stylized reproduction of ordinary human action, such as heavy breathing, slicing vegetables, sobbing, or playing the shamisen, 51, 57

geta (thonged wooden clogs): *see* stage clogs

geza, see offstage-music room

Gidayū (Takemoto), narrator (1651–1714); established the style of narration of the puppet drama and founded the Takemoto-za, 7

gidayū, gidayū bushi: narrative storytelling, lyrical chanting of puppet drama in the style of Gidayū, 7

gidayū shamisen (storytelling shamisen): the large, thick-necked shamisen used in Bunraku and for all *gidayū*- or *jōruri*-type accompaniment, 4

Gihei, character in *Katsuragawa Renri no Shigarami,* 153

gloves, 27, 51, 163

glue, 115–16

gofun, see gesso

greetings, among troupe members, 61, 134–36

Hachirobei (Tatsumatsu), puppeteer (d. 1734), 7

Hadesugata Onna Maiginu (*The Courtesan's Colorful Dance Robe,* 1772), play by Takemoto Saburōbei et al. about the merchant Hanshichi, his wife Osono, and his lover Sankatsu, 120

hair, human, 102–3; wax (*bintsuke*), 103; yak, 103; *see also* wigs

hakama (pleated, divided skirt): worn in various combinations by puppeteers, narrators, and musicians, originally part of the formal wear of the Edo period, 32, 33, 34, 61, *146*, 163; worn by puppets in some roles, 119; *see also,* costume; *tayū*; shamisen players

hands, puppet, 93, 98, 108, 117, 118; octopus-grip, 117; of puppeteers, 58, 90, 94, 149; *see also* Hishida; Ōe

Hangan, character in *Chūshingura,* 56
hara, see abdomen
hara-kiri (ritual suicide by blade): *see* suicide
hara maki, see belly band
hara obi, see belly sash
hayaku: category of head used for minor or supporting male roles, 92
headband, copper, *see* copper headband
headgear, *see* props
headgrip (*dōgushi*): wooden stick, to which neck and head of puppet are permanently attached, from which toggles connected to the inside of the head protrude, and which is held by chief or one-man puppeteer with his left hand, 32, 90, 93, 94, 97, 98, 100, 106, *109,* 115, 124
head inspection, 56, 64, 65, *145,* 154, 166
head puppeteer (*omo-zukai*): also, chief puppeteer; the puppeteer who operates head and right arm, 9, 34
heads, puppet (*kashira*), 100, *107;* carving of, 93–96, *109;* carving by Hishida, 118; construction of, 97–98, *107;* distributor of, selection by, 87–92; female puppets, 88, 89, 92, 94, 116, 118, 126, 127; male puppets, 92, 95, 98, 99, 115, 116; painting of, 106, *111,* 115–18; repair of, 106, 115–18; severed, 130, 131, *139;* storage of, 87–92, 159; types of, 55, 87–92, 115–18
hechima, see loofah
heel grips (*ashigane*): cloth-wrapped metal strips attached to puppets' feet at the heel and grasped by foot operator, 51, 53, 116, 154
Heike Nyogo no Shima (The Heike Island of Exile, 1719) historical play by Chikamatsu Monzaemon, 56

hem (*suso*), used to suggest leg movement of female puppets, 51, 54, 126
hidari-zukai, see left-arm manipulator
hinoki, see cypress, Japanese
hips, of puppeteers, 53, 54, 58; of puppets, *113,* 124, 125
Hiragana Seisuiki (Chronicles of Decline and Prosperity, 1739), historical play by Takeda Izumo et al., 93, 94
Hishida, Kōji, keeper, repairer, and painter of heads, 91, 98, 106, 111, 115–118, *145*
historical dramas, *see* plays, historical
honorifics, used in speech among troupe members, 135, 171
hood (*zukin*): black cotton or linen semi-transparent head covering reaching midchest level that is always worn on stage by left-arm manipulators and leg operators, except in a very few specific scenes, and often also by the chief puppeteer, 9, 29, 30, 32, 34, 164; different styles, 47; Kiritake hood, *143;* padded, for packing heads, 145, 161, 166
hooded puppeteers (*kage-zukai*): left-arm manipulators, leg operators, and one-man puppet operators always wear hoods while performing, while chief puppeteers are hooded in only some scenes, 10; *see also* hood
"hundred-days' growth" wig, 101, *110,* *145,* 161
hyōshigi (also *ki*), *see* clappers
Hyōsuke, blind character in *Gokusaishiki Musume Ōgi, (The Maiden's Colorful Fan,* 1746), a play by Chikamatsu Hanji, 52

"Ikudama Shrine" scene (*Sonezaki Shinjū*), 16–18, *19–20,* 27–30, *142* "important intangible cultural property" (*jūyō mukei bunkazai*): an official designation by the Japanese government; the Osaka Bunraku Troupe as a group holder thereof, 9; *see also* "living national treasure"

instruments, musical (other than shamisen): from the Ryukyus, 3; *kokyū*, 10; koto, 10, 78

interval (*ma*): musical term, 66

iron, *113*, 122, 123

Ishibashi, Osamu, costume director (*ishōbu*), *112*, 119–23, 161

Itchō (Kiritake), puppeteer, *46, 47, 49, 115*, 156, 158

Japan Broadcasting Corporation, 6; *see also* NHK

jidaimono, see plays, historical

jōen shiryōshū: booklets issued by the national theatres of Tokyo and Osaka containing extensive information about plays being performed in the current Bunraku runs at those theatres, 159

Jōruri, Princess, legendary beauty loved by Genji warrior Minamoto Yoshitsune and celebrated in *The Tale of Princess Jōruri*, 3

jōruri: general name for puppet drama, as well as specific name for the musical narrative of the genre, 4

journey (*michiyuki*): travel, usually of lovers, depicted in a dancelike scene in many Bunraku plays, 10, 15, 17, 24–26; see also *Sonezaki Shinjū;* suicide

Jūzō (Tsuruzawa), shamisen player, *73*, 77–81, 156

Kabuki, viii, 4, 5, 16, 121, 148; actors, ix; puppet dramas performed as, viii

kaishaku, see stage assistant

Kanematsu IV (Kiritake), puppeteer, *49*, 155–56, 158, 166–67

kamishimo (Edo-period formal dress): costume consisting of a *kataginu* and *hakama* over a plain, black (or, in summer, white) crested kimono worn by *tayū*, shamisen players, and occasionally also by chief puppeteers, 15, 34, 60, 61, *67–72*

Kanadehon Chūshingura (*The Forty-Seven Rōnin*, 1748) historical play by Takeda Izumo, Miyoshi Shōraku, and Namiki Sōsuke about the "loyal forty-seven" *rōnin*, (masterless samurai) that was written for puppets and later adapted for Kabuki actors; often referred to as *Chūshingura*, 56, 91

Kanji VI (Tsuruzawa), shamisen player (1887–1974) and "living national treasure," 64, 75

Kanjū (Kiritake), puppeteer, 136–37

Kanjūrō (Kiritake), puppeteer, 10, 87, *145,* 152–54; casting plays, 151; "living national treasure," 158

Kanshūsai, character in *Sugawara Denju Tenarai Kagami*, 92

kashira, see heads, puppet

kashirawari iin, see heads, selection of; *see also* Bunjaku

Kashiwagi, Takayuki, stage assistant for the yuka, 62, 162

kata, see pose

kataginu, see vest

kata ita, see shoulder board

Katsuragawa Renri no Shigarami, (*The Love Story of Ohan and Chōemon,* 1776), play by Suga Sensuke, often referred to as simply *Katsuragawa,* xii, 95, 130

katsura, katsura-ya, see wig, wig master

Kawashima, Toshimichi, prop assistant, 132, 139

kazura, kazura-ya, see wig, wig master

keisei, see courtesan

Keisei Hangonkō (*Matahei the Stutterer,* 1708) play by Chikamatsu Monzaemon, 32

Kembishi: type of puppet head based on the character in *Yōmei Tennō Shokunin* (1705), by Chikamatsu Monzaemon, 89, 91, 92, 95, 98

kendai, see lectern

ki, see wooden clappers

Kichibei IX (Nozawa), shamisen player (1903–80), 62, 63, 75, 163, 165–67

kimono, performers,' 31, 34; puppeteers, 18, 28, 34; shamisen player's, 15, 32; tayū's, 15, 32, 61; *see also* costume

Kineya, Hyōji, offstage musician, 83–86

Kinshi IV (Nozawa), shamisen player, *74*

Kintoki: type of male puppet head based on a villain in *Ōeyama Shutendōji* (1854) depicted with round eyes, dark complexion, and a mean expression, 92

kiri, see paulownia

Kiritake (literally, "paulownia bamboo"): surname of many puppeteers; style of puppeteers' hoods, 47

Kizaemon II (Nozawa), shamisen player (1891–1976), 136

knees, of puppets, 53, 54

kodōgu, kodōgu-ya, see props, prop master

Kokuritsu Bunraku Gekijō, see The National Bunraku Theatre of Osaka

Kokuritsu Gekijō, see The National Theatre of Tokyo

Kokusen'ya Kassen (*The Battles of Coxinga,* 1715) a historical play by Chikamatsu Monzaemon, 8, 47

kokyū: small bowed instrument, 10

Komatsudayū (Toyotake), narrator, 147–48, 158

Kōmei: type of puppet head based on the character in *Shokatsu Kōmei Kanae Gundan* (1724), by Takeda Izumo, 88

Koshijidayū IV (Takemoto), narrator, 10, 66, *69*, 138, 147; as a "living national treasure," 158

Kotama (Yoshida): former stage name of puppeteer Bungo, 32–33

Kōtarō, character in *Sugawara Denju Tenarai Kagami*, 92, 165

Kōtsubodayū II (Toyotake), narrator (1878–1967); also known by title Yamashiro (no) Shōjō bestowed by imperial family, 63

kotsuzumi: hourglass-shaped drum used in the *geza* and played at shoulder level, 82–86

kowarichō, see role-assignment book

kozaru, see toggles

kuchibari, see mouth pin

Kuheiji, character in *Sonezaki Shinjū,* 16, 28–30, 92, 95

kujira no hige, see baleen

kuroko, kurogo, see robe

laughing, narrator's mastery of, 150

lectern (*kendai*): reading stand used by the tayū to hold his text or script and usually ornately lacquered, 15, 17, 60, *67, 71, 72,* 162, 164

left-arm manipulator (*hidari-zukai*): the second puppeteer of the Bunraku trio who uses his right arm to operate the puppet's left arm by means of a rod, the *sashigane,* attached to the puppet's left arm, and assists the chief puppeteer by handing props to him as necessary, 34–35, *36–37,* 55, 117, 131

legless female puppets, 51, 54, 57

leg operator (*ashi-zukai*): third and most junior puppeteer who manipulates the puppet's legs or moves the hem of the costume for legless female puppets to give the illusion of movement, 36–37, 51, 56, 126, 131, 149; training, 54; *see also* legs

legs, puppet, 53–55, 56, 93, 98, 116, 117, 124, 128, 154–55, 161

licensed quarters (*kuruwa*): specific areas in cities, licensed by the government, with "teahouses" and houses of assignation for use by prostitutes and their customers, 15, 83, 88

limbs, severed, *see* props

lines, on puppet faces, 115

lion, mythical (*oshishi*): mask or carved head used in various dances, 94

lips, *22*, 95, 115, 116; *see also* mouth pin

"living national treasure" (*ningen kokuhō*): individuals designated *jūyō mukei bunkazai hojisha* ("holder of an important intangible cultural asset") are popularly referred to as *ningen kokuhō*, or "living national treasures"; in the Bunraku troupe currently, puppeteers Tamao and Kanjūrō, *tayū* Koshijidayū and Tsudayū, and shamisen player Enza, 9, 55, 58, 158; the Osaka troupe is designated, as a group, a *jūyō mukei bunkazai*, or an "important intangible cultural asset," 9

loofah (*hechima*): dried gourd that provides the spongelike material sewn to the shoulder board to create the puppet's shoulder line, 125; *see also* shoulder board

The Love Story of Ohan and Chōemon (*Katsuragawa Renri no Shigarami*, 1776), play by Suga Sensuke, xii, 95, 130

The Love Suicides at Sonezaki, (*Sonezaki Shinjū*, 1703) play by Chikamatsu Monzaemon, viii–ix, xii, 4, 5, 8, 13, 15–18, *19–26*, 27–32, 57, 92, 95, *142, 143*; veranda scene, viii, 16, *22, 143*

lovers' suicide (*shinjū*), 17, *22*, 130; *see also* suicide; journey

ma, see interval

mae goshirae ("making ahead"): creation or assembling of puppet; also *ningyō tsukuri*, 124–28

master (*shishō*): an honorific used by junior performers or apprentices to or about their teacher or instructor, 118

Matahei The Stutterer (*Keisei Hangonkō*, 1708), play by Chikamatsu Monzaemon, 32

Matsuōmaru, character in *Sugawara Denju Tenarai Kagami*, 56, 91, 92, 110, 117, 119, 120; Kanjūrō performing role of, *145*; puppet on tour, 161; Tamao performing role of, 165–67; Tsudayū narrating role of, 165–67

melody (*fushi*): musical statement or lyrical narration, 66

Mentholatum, used by shamisen players, 80

messengers, role in plays, 154

michiyuki, see journey

Midoridayū (Takemoto): narrator, 61–62, 75, 148, 163

Ministry of Education, (Cultural Affairs Agency), 6

mino, see cape

Minoshi (Yoshida), puppeteer, 164

Minosuke III (Yoshida), puppeteer, 9, *21–26*, 30–31, *38*, 53, 125–27, 155, 164

Minotarō (Yoshida), puppeteer, 35, *143*, 154–55

misu, see bamboo blinds

Mitsuwa-kai, 6

Mochizuki, Haruo, offstage musician, 82–86

Mochizuki, Taishirō, offstage musician, *74*, 82–86, 162, 165, 167

Mojitayū IX (Takemoto), narrator, 150 158

Monju (Kiritake), puppeteer, *143*

Monjūrō II (Kiritake), puppeteer (1900–1970), xiii, 86, 127, 136, 148, 153

Mon'ya (Kiritake), puppeteer now named Tamamatsu III; *see* Tamamatsu

Monzō II (Kiritake), puppeteer (1880–1948), 94

mouth, 115

mouth pin (*kuchibari*, "mouth needle"): thin nail, pin, or needle inserted in the lower lip of some female puppets; the puppeteer catches the puppet's sleeve or hand towel on the pin for stylized gestures of grief, *22*, 116

movements, puppet, *see* gestures; poses

mu, see nothingness

museum, Bunraku, 7, 14

musicians, *see* offstage musicians; shamisen players

musume, see young woman

naka eri, see neckband

Nakoshi, Shōji, wig master and hairdresser, 100–105, *109, 110,* 115, 118, *145,* 161, 162, 166, 167

Nambudayū (Takemoto), narrator, 32

names, stage or professional, xiii, 148

narrators (*tayū*): narrative and lyrical storyteller, chanter, 4–5, 9, 10, 15, 17–18, 27, 29–30, 32, 56, 60–66, *67–72,* 76, 80–81, 85, 138–39, 147–48, 150, 157, 163, 165

National Bunraku Theatre, Osaka (Kokuritsu Bunraku Gekijō): also, National Bunraku Theatre of Japan, xi, 6, 7, 14, *19,* 87, 132–33, 158–59

National Theatre of Japan, Tokyo (Kokuritsu Gekijō, Tokyo): comprises theatres for performance of Kabuki, Bunraku, and, in separate buildings, for Rakugo (comic storytelling) and Nō, xiii, 8, 87, 140–41

neck, 97, *109*

neckband (*eri* or *naka eri*): a padded or flat strip of material attached to the puppet's shoulder board as the foundation of the costume; also, a strip attached to the inner and outer kimonos which are placed over the separate neckbands attached first, *113,* 123, 125, 126, 127, 128

needles, x, 52, 121–23, 126; mouth, *22,* 116

The New Ballad Singer (Shimpan Utazaimon, 1780) a play by Chikamatsu Hanji, 130

NHK (Nihon Hōsō Kyōkai), *see* Japan Broadcasting Corporation

ni chō: "two clacks"; *see* clappers

nii-san: "older brother," an honorific used for seniors, 135

ningyō jōruri: doll, or puppet, storytelling; the general term for narrative puppet dramas in Japan, 4

ningyō-zukai, see puppeteer

nodding string (*unazuki no ito*), 160, *109,* 115; *see also* toggle, main

notebooks (*tsukechō*): for costume director, 121, 123; offstage musicians' (cue book), 84, 85; prop men, 132; role book, 151–52

nothingness (*mu*): emptiness, void, selflessness (a Buddhist term), 65, 147–48

obi: sash worn over the kimono by men and women; courtesan's, 126; male puppet's, 52; *see also* belly sash octopus-grip hands (*tako tsukami*): fully articulated male puppet hands, 117, 118

Ōe, Minosuke, carver of heads, 93–99, *107–9*, 117, 118

offstage music and musicians (*geza*): the music played in a small room above the stage-right entrance curtain to enhance the mood of the play and to create sound effects; the room itself; also, the musicians who play the drums, flutes, gongs, whistles, etc. in the offstage music room, *74*, 82–86, *140*, 162, 164, 165, 167

Ofuku: type of female puppet head, 92

Ohan, character in *Katsuragawa Renri no Shigarami*, xii, 130

Ohatsu, character in *Sonezaki Shinjū*, viii, 16–31, *19, 21–26*, 57, 92

oiran: top-ranking courtesan; see courtesan

ojii, see old man

old man (*ojii*): type of puppet head, 89

old woman (*baba*): type of puppet head, 88

Omitsu, character in *Shimpan Utazaimon*, 130

omo-zukai, see head puppeteer

one-man puppets (*tsume*): simple puppets used for roles as messengers, ladies-in-waiting, constables, warriors, maids, etc., 5, 9, 51, 91, 92, 95, *139*, 151, 154–55

Osaka Bunraku Troupe, 6, 8

oshishi, mythical lion, 69

Osono, character in *Hadesugata Onna Maiginu*, 120

Otama, 92

otoshi, see bag, narrator's

packing cases (*bote*): wooden-framed burlap cases used to transport puppets, equipment, and performers' clothing, etc. on tour, *145*, 160, 161, 162, 166, 167

paint and painting, of puppets, 58, 106, *111*, 115

partitions, stage (*tesuri*): three sets of low, horizontal partitions ranging from about eleven to thirty-three inches in height that divide the stage into three areas and partially hide the puppeteers from the audience's view, *20*, 82, 85, 131, 160

paulownia (*kiri*): a tree and its soft wood, used for puppet limbs, the heads of one-man puppets, and occasionally for puppet heads, 95, 98, 99

performance gown (*kuroko, kurogo*), *see* robe

pillow, narrator's, *see* bag

platform, revolving, *see* auxiliary stage

plays, choice of, 87

plays, domestic (*sewamono*): plays dealing with the everyday life of the ordinary people, usually the townspeople of the Edo period and often tragedies, 4, 8, 147; see also *Hadesugata Onna Maiginu, Katsuragawa Renri no Shigarami, Sonezaki Shinjū*

plays, historical (*jidaimono*): plays based, often loosely, on historical or legendary events and personages, often featuring flamboyant costumes, sets, and performances, 4, 147; see also *Ashiya Dōman Ōuchi Kagami, Chūshingura, Heike Nyogo no Shima, Hiragana Seisuiki, Kokusen'ya Kassen, Sugawara Denju Tenarai Kagami*

plectrum (*bachi*), thick, blunt-ended ivory striking instrument used to hit strings and skin head of soundbox and pluck

the strings of the shamisen, 17, 76–81
poison, in Bunraku plays, 130
pose (*kata*): a temporarily frozen position or a series of stylized movements performed in sequence to emphasize the puppet's form (male) or beauty (female) or to accentuate a dramatic or emotional climax, 51, 54, 57, 153, 163
powder, arrowroot for shamisen neck, 80; rice-straw ash for hold on plectrum, 80
prayer, 61, 62, *70, 72*
programs, printed, 159
prompt book, *see* role-assignment book
prop man (*kodōgu-ya*), *see* props
props (*kodōgu*): hand and stage props, headgear, footgear, conveyances, animals, severed heads and limbs, 32, 129–133, *139*; animals, 130–32; flowers, 130, 131; food, 130; foxes, 130, 132, *139*; puppeteers' training with and use of, 51, 53, 131, *139*, 151, 153, 155; severed heads, 130, 131, *139*; severed limbs, 130; size of, 131; tables (*rendai*), 131; on tour, 162, 166; *see also* prop man, prop stands
prop stands (*rendai*): simple black wooden stands hidden from the audience by stage partitions, used only when a prop is in actual use and moved on, off, and about the stage by a junior puppeteer stage assistant (*kaishaku*), prop man, or assistant; also used by puppeteers under feet of puppets to support weight during long, fairly stationary scenes, 131; *see also* props
prostitute (*keisei* or *oiran*), *see* courtesan
puppeteers (*ningyō-zukai*), see head puppeteer (*omo-zukai*); left-arm manipulator (*hidari-zukai*); leg operator (*ashi-zukai*)

quince (*karin*): wood used for some shamisen bodies, 77

rain cape (*mino*), *see* cape
reading stand (*kendai*), *see* lectern
red dye (*beni*): made from the petals of safflower, 120, 121
rehearsals, stage or dress (*keiko* or *butai-geiko*), *20–26, 35–37, 42–45, 49,* 51, *67, 73,* 85, *140–44,* 149–151, *157*
rendai, see prop stand
rivalry, among performers, 66, 150
robe, of puppeteers, (*kuroko, kurogo*): black cotton, long-sleeved, ankle-length rehearsal robe or performance gown that closes with kimonolike crossover at chest and ties over right hip and is worn by all puppeteers for stage rehearsals, by left-arm manipulators, leg operators, and one-man puppet operators for stage performances, and, in slightly varied style, by stage assistants and stagehands, 34, 135, 163
role-assignment book (*kowarichō*): for casting (also cue book), 150–52

safflower (*benibana*): source of red dye used for fabrics and cosmetics, 121
Sakujūrō (Yoshida), puppeteer, 40, 128, *143*
salaries, 158
salt, 163
samisen, *see* shamisen
sandals, puppeteers' (zori): worn in wings by chief puppeteers before changing to stage clogs, and, of a simpler straw type, by left-arm manipulators, leg operators, *kaishaku,* other stage assistants, and stagehands, *20,* 31, 34, *38–40, 46–48, 50,* 51, 136, *139*; also

waraji, straw sandals used in pairs to sole stage clogs, 36, 34, *38–42, 46–48, 50,* 51, *139, 142*

sandalwood, 77

sashigane, see armature

seamstress, *see* Uehara, Tsuruko

Seijūrō IV (Toyomatsu), puppeteer (1926–84), 163, 165, 167

Seinosuke (Toyomatsu), puppeteer, 72, 156

Seitomo (Tsuruzawa), shamisen player, 164–65

selflessness (*mu*), 65, 147–58

seniority, 10, 148

seppuku, see suicide

sets, stage, 31, *19–21, 23, 38–43, 47–49, 139–44,* 160

sewamono, see plays, domestic

shamisen (often spelled samisen): a three stringed, banjo-shaped musical instrument; that used in Bunraku, called the *gidayu* shamisen, is the largest and has the thickest neck, 10, 17–18, 27–30, 32, *67, 71, 72, 74,* 75, 76–81; 85, 163–64; bridges, 76, 77; introduction of, 3; life span, 152; puppeteer's comments on, 56; strings used in puppets, 97, *108, 109,* 117, 118; *tayū*'s comments on, 62–64; trainees, 156–57; tuning of, 77–78, 163–64

shells, for sound effects, 83; *see also* gesso

Shikoku, 83, 91, 94; tour of, 160–167

Shimpan Utazaimon (*The New Ballad Singer,* 1780) a play by Chikamatsu Hanji, 130

shinjū, see suicide

shishō, see master

Shōchiku Theatrical Company, 6, 121

shoulder board (*kata ita*): a wooden board that serves as the puppet's shoulders and, with strips of loofah attached at the ends and with cloth or heavy paper attached in front and back into the ends of which is inserted a bamboo hoop to represent hips, forms the understructure (*dō*) of the puppet to which pieces of costume are sewn to create a puppet for a specific role, *113,* 124, 125, 127

Shunkan, character in *Heike Nyogo no Shima,* 56

silk, *see* costumes; shamisen strings

socks (*tabi*): bifurcated socks worn by all performers; white *tabi* worn by chief puppeteers when in kimonos, by shamisen players, and by *tayū*; black by left-arm manipulators, leg operators, one-man puppet operators, stage assistants, and stagehands; also worn by some puppets, 61, 128; *see also* left-arm manipulator, leg operator, stage assistants, and stagehands

Sonezaki Shinjū (*The Love Suicides at Sonezaki,* 1703): domestic tragedy by Chikamatsu Monzaemon

stage, 15, *19, 20,* 34, *38–47,* 82, *140–42*

stage, auxiliary (*yuka*), *see* auxiliary stage

stage assistant (*kaishaku*): junior puppeteer, hooded and almost completely hidden from the audience by stage partitions, who assists puppeteers, *47, 48,* 131, 136, *142, 144,* 155, 151–52; also, men specifically assigned to assist during rehearsals and backstage, such as Suzuki, Kōji, 160, 167; and with *tayū*'s lecterns, such as Kashiwagi, Takayuki, 62, 162

stage clogs (*butai geta*): high (five- to over twelve-inch) wooden clogs, soled with two straw sandals, worn by the chief puppeteer to raise him above the other operators for ease of movement, and very occasionally, such as for the role of Matsuōmaru in the "Terakoya" scene of *Sugawara Denju Tenarai Kagami,* by the left-arm operator, 10, 31, 32, 41, 46, *139,* 149, 164, 165, 167; accidents on, 55; moved by junior puppeteer for chief puppeteer, 152

stage curtain, main (*jōshiki maku*): black, green, and terracotta striped curtain drawn from right to left, 15, 30

stage-entrance curtains (*komaku*): black curtains, with white designs of the Takemoto and Toyotake crests, attached to rods with heavy rings, set at angles on stage right and stage left and pulled open and closed by puppeteers for stage entrances by puppets, 4, 17, 53, 140, 165

stagehands, 31, *39, 40, 46, 48, 139–42,* 160, 164

stage names, *see* names

stage partitions (*tesuri*), *see* partitions

stands, bamboo, *see* bamboo; *see also* props

sticks (*tsuke*), *see* clappers; (*tsukiage bō*), *see* support sticks

stools (*shirihiki,* also *shichibei, aibiki*): miniature seat used by *tayū* on the *yuka,* 62, 68

strings, of puppet heads, 34, 52, 97, 98, *109;* of shamisen, 76; used in wings, 103, 104; *see also* heads; toggles

Sugawara Denju Tenarai Kagami (Sugawara's Secrets of Calligraphy, 1746), play by Takeda Izumo et al., loosely based on the life of Sugawara Michizane, tenth-century statesman; one of the most famous and often-performed plays of the Bunraku repertory, *39, 42–43, 45,* 56, 62, 64, 91, 92, 95, 115, 154; costumes for, 119, 120, 122; hands

for Matsuōmaru, 117; head for Matsuōmaru, *110;* heads for tour, *145;* Kanjūrō in role of Matsuōmaru in the "Terakoya" scene, *145;* props, 130; on tour, 160–68

suicide (hara-kiri and *seppuku*): ritual disembowelment, 10, 15, 35, 56, 57, 130, 153; hair loosened during, 104; (*shinjū*): lovers' suicide, 17, *22;* in river, 130

Sumitayū, *see* Mojitayū

support sticks (*tsukiage bō*): bamboo stick attached to right side of shoulder board of most male puppets and sometimes rested on chief puppeteer's right hip to redistribute weight of a heavy doll during long stationary scenes or to make strenuous movements by the puppet easier to perform, *113*

Suzuki, Kōji, stage assistant who assists with flats, sets, and the *yuka,* also acting as stage carpenter on tours, 13, 167

tabi, see socks

Takemoto crest, iv, 17, *140–41,* 165

Takemoto Gidayū (1651–1714), narrator who established the leading style of narration for puppet drama and founded the Takemoto Theatre in 1684, 4; see also *gidayū*

Takemoto Theatre (Takemoto-za), 5, 8

tako tsukami (literally, "octopus grip"): fully articulated male puppet hands, 117, 118

Tamagorō (Yoshida), puppeteer, 32–33, *50*

Tamaichi II (Yoshida), puppeteer, (1894–1965), 91, 148

Tamaichirō (Yoshida), puppeteer, 149; *see also* Tamamatsu III

Tamaki (Yoshida), puppeteer, 52

Tamakō (Yoshida), puppeteer, 129

Tamamatsu II (Yoshida), puppeteer (1885–1948); later called Tamasuke, Tamaichi II, and Tamazō IV, 52

Tamamatsu III (Yoshida), puppeteer (son of Tamazō IV), xiii, 94, *113,* 148–150

Tamame (Yoshida), puppeteer, 20, *146,* 164, 165

Tamanosuke (Yoshida), puppeteer and prop assistant, 132, 133

Tamao (Yoshida), puppeteer, 10, *19–20, 22–26,* 31, *41, 49,* 51–59, 87, 91, 118, 127; casting a play, 151; directing, *142, 143, 144;* "living national treasure," 158; as Matsuōmaru, 119, 165–67

Tamashō (Yoshida), puppeteer (1878–1983), 165, 167

Tamasuke III (Yoshida), *see* Tamamatsu II

Tamazō IV (Yoshida), *see* Tamamatsu II

Tatsumatsu, Hachirobei, puppeteer (d. 1734), 5

tayū, see narrator

"Teahouse" scene, *see* "Temmaya Teahouse" scene

television, 8, 11

"Temmaya Teahouse" scene, from *Sonezaki Shinjū,* viii, 16, *21–26*

"Temple School" scene, see "Terakoya" scene

"Terakoya" (temple school) scene: the "Village School" scene, a scene from *Sugawara Denju Tenarai Kagami,* 56, 62, 92, *145,* 160–68

tesuri, see partitions, stage

third-generation performers, 148, 158

toggles: for the operation of puppet heads and also some puppet arms and hands; arm toggles, in the right arm and the armature controlling the left hand, *36, 37, 108,* 117; hand toggles, 117; main toggle (*choi*): a wooden toggle that slides in a channel carved into the front of the headgrip and is operated by the chief puppeteer between middle and ring fingers of his left hand. It is connected by a used shamisen string, or "nodding string" (*unazuki no ito*), to the inside of the puppet head and raises and lowers the head in a nodding action, 34, 52, 97, 98, 100, 106, 161; small toggles (*kozaru*): the small wood or bamboo toggles, as many as five, attached to the back of the headgrip and operated by the chief puppeteer's thumb. They are connected with silk or cotton cord to workings inside the puppet head to make eyes open, close, turn, and cross, eyebrows rise and fall, mouths open and close, and to create other effects 87, 97–98, 115, 161

Tokubei, character in *Sonezaki Shinjū,* viii–ix, 16–18, *19–20, 22–26,* 27–31, 32, 57, 92, *143*

Tokutayū (Toyotake), narrator, 32

Tonami, character in *Sugawara Denju Tenarai Kagami,* 92, 161, 162, 165–67

tours, xii, 11, 91, *145, 146,* 160–68

Toyotake crest, iv, 17, *140–41,* 165

Toyotake Theatre (Toyotake-za), 5

tōzai ("east and west"): "Hear ye!" The call of the puppeteer who announces the performers of each scene or sub-scene before it commences, 17, 151

training, of Bunraku artists, 52–53, 65, 79, 130, 137, 149, 154–55, 157; *see also* individual artists

training course, at National Theatre, 9, 52, 65, 156–57, 158–59
Tsudayū III (Takemoto, 1869–1941), narrator, 63
Tsudayū IV (Takemoto), narrator, 10, 60–66, *70–71*, 75, 87, 163, 165–67; "living national treasure," 158
tsuke, see clappers
tsukechō, see notebooks
tsukiage bō, see support stick
tsume, see one-man puppet
tuning: drums, 83–85; shamisen (*chōshi*), 76, 77–78, 163

Uehara, Tsuruko, seamstress, *113,* 121–23
Uemura Bunrakuken, *see* Bunrakuken
unazuki no ito, see nodding string
urakata ("people in the back"): craftsmen and other backstage workers such as costume director, head repairer, off-stage musicians, prop men, wig master, seamstress, stage assistants, and stage-hands, who do not appear on stage during performances; *see* specific chapters
usu tamago ("light egg"): beige shade of paint used usually for rustic characters, old men, or men with a mean streak, 116

veranda scene (from *The Love Suicides of Sonezaki*), viii, *22,* 35, *143*
vest (*kataginu*): a stiff, sleeveless formal shoulder covering worn over the top of the kimono with the *hakama*; the vest and the *hakama* comprise the *kamishimo*, the Edo-period formal cos-tume worn by narrators and shamisen players in performance, and, in special scenes, also by chief puppeteers in performance; *see* costumes
"Village School" scene, *see* "Terakoya" scene

Wada, Tokiyo, prop man, 132–33
waka otoko, see young male
Wakatama, (Yoshida), puppeteer, *33*
wax (*bintsuke*), 103
whalebone, *see* baleen
whale's beard, *see* baleen
whistles, 84–85
The White Fox of Shinoda Wood, (*Ashiya Dōman Ōuchi Kagami,* 1734), play by Takeda Izumo, 8, 99, *139*
wigs (*kazura*); wig master (*kazura-ya,* also, *tokoyama*), 100–105, *109, 110,* 115; *see also* Nakoshi, Shōji
wooden clappers, *see* clappers
wrists, of puppets, 53

yak hair, *x,* 103
Yamashiro (no) Shōjō, see Kōtsubodayū II
Yasuna, character in *Ashiya Dōman Ōuchi Kagami,* 99
Yokambei: type of puppet head based on a character in *Ashiya Dōman Ōuchi Kagami,* 94
Yonetani, Eijirō, prop man (retired), 129–32
young man (*waka otoko*), type of role and puppet head, 88
young woman (*musume*): type of role and puppet head, 88, 92, 95, 101
yuka, see auxiliary stage

zori, *see* sandals
zukin, see hood

The "weathermark" identifies this book as a production of John Weatherhill, Inc., publishers of fine books on Asia and the Pacific. Editorial supervision: Jeffrey Hunter. Book design and typography: Miriam F. Yamaguchi. Layout of illustrations: Yutaka Shimoji. Production supervision: Mitsuo Okado. Composition of the text, in letterpress: Korea Textbook Co., Seoul. Printing of the text: Shobundo Printing Co., Tokyo. Engraving and printing of the plates, in monochrome offset: Nissha Printing Co., Kyoto. The typeface used is Monotype Baskerville.